# The Three Sisters
## QUICK AND EASY
### INDIAN COOKBOOK

To mum,
for your love and inspiration

# The Three Sisters
# QUICK AND EASY
# INDIAN COOKBOOK

*Delicious, authentic recipes to make at home*

FLAVOURS AND SPICES OF INDIA

## SEREENA, ALEXA & PRIYA KAUL

First published in Great Britain by
Simon and Schuster UK Ltd, 2012
A CBS Company

© Abacus Publishing Limited

Design and new photography copyright © Simon and
Schuster UK Ltd

SIMON AND SCHUSTER
ILLUSTRATED BOOKS

Simon & Schuster UK
222 Gray's Inn Road
London  WC1X 8HB
www.simonandschuster.co.uk

A CIP catalogue record of this book is available from the
British Library.

The right of Abacus Publishing Limited to be identified
as the Author of this Work has been asserted by them
in accordance with sections 77 and 78 of the Copyright,
Designs and Patents Act, 1988.

10 9 8 7 6 5 4 3 2 1

Commercial Director: Ami Richards
Senior Commissioning Editor: Nicky Hill
Project Editor: Abi Waters
Design: Corinna Farrow
Production Manager: Katherine Thornton
Photography: William Shaw
Home economist: Kate Blinman
Stylist: Liz Hippisley

Printed and bound in China

ISBN 978-1-47111-347-5

**Recipe notes:**
All teaspoons and tablespoons are level.
All spice spoons are rounded and 1 spice spoon is
equivalent to ½ teaspoon.
All cooking times are approximate and will vary in
accordance with the type of cooker hob, conventional or
fan oven used.
As you familiarize yourself with the recipes, feel free
to experiment with the amount of chilli used to suit
your taste.
Please be advised this book includes recipes where nuts
have been used.

*Parychai*

Introduction

# Chaar Rasoi

## The Four Kitchens

We had such a huge success with our first book, *The Three Sister's Indian Cookbook* that it only seemed right for us to go one step further and bring on and develop your interest by extending our repertoire again with this new book of Quick and Easy Indian Recipes.

India is a large country with vast climate changes and a wide-ranging cuisine from the north to south and east to west. The very north of India use dried fennel to thicken their sauces while further south, in Punjab and Delhi, it is coriander with onions; southern Indians prefer to use a creamy coconut base to do the same. The unique final flavouring of most south Indian food comes from the leaves of the curry tree. North Indian cuisine has been greatly influenced by invaders on its border, particularly the Mughals who gave India rich and exotic biryanis, kebabs and tikkas. East Indian cuisine features a variety of fish and prawn dishes with a light touch of spice, making them appealing to all, accompanied by a delectable number of chutneys. Food is also preferred steamed like the ever popular *momos* (vegetable- or chicken-filled dumpling) that appears on street food stalls. East Indian desserts are known to be the best in India with endless varieties in existence. Over in the west of India, a more varied cuisine exists, including Goan dishes of coconut, red chillies and vinegar; Gujrat has the most interesting snack foods like pappadoms and vegetarian dishes, while in the Mumbai region the curries are sour and spicy.

In this book we have given a lot of attention to the south of India where it is generally hot in temperature and many foods have to ferment overnight before being cooked like *idali* and *dosa* (steamed cake-shaped and pancake-style dal and rice mixture). We are aware that in today's world, everybody wants a variety of fast recipes, from all the regions and we have put our three heads together and done just that.

*Sereena, Alexa and Priya Kaul*

# Redhi Wala

## Street Food Vendors

Street food is a phenomenon in warmer parts of India and is carried out by vendors with their food and cooking ware on hand-drawn carts. What is amazing is that it is so inexpensive and tasty. An abundance of business is carried out on a daily basis, much of which is probably unaccounted for by the Indian revenue offices! Thank god for this, because within minutes a plate of rice can be placed in your hand with two forks dug in, even before you have time to decide on the preference of sauces. What we like about street food, apart from the tasty cuisine, is that you never feel alone when eating with a street full of people.

The big cities have a larger variety of street food on stalls and so it becomes impossible to walk through a busy street and not buy a hot samosa, have two sips of stewed masala chai, a small plate of fruit chaat or just a cool drink of coconut water.

People all over India love food cooked in front of them just on the edge of the street; it's as though the restaurant was brought to them instead of having to go into one. If you don't feel like an Indian-Chinese (you can come across a wonderful fusion of this), then just keep walking and sure enough, at the next corner, a man will be baling up *laacha parathas* in front of you. Don't try to make too much conversation, these professionals have to feed hoards of people, but do watch how they cook. Their artful techniques are mastered over many years, probably from the time they came looking for work on the streets. It's a joy to watch a chef throw a *rumali roti* (muslin-thin flatbread) in the air and then toss it over an upside-down *kadhai* (wok-type pan).

When we're in India, colours come into being; the fabrics worn by people and the food they eat; the colourful yellow dals, red tandoori chicken, brown chapatis and pink burfi. To add to this, we develop a carefree attitude where time matters not; we remember why we love India! The sun sets early, there is still a hustle and bustle on the streets, and you can hear the chanting of mantras in nearby temples. A fragrance of incense develops and is seen oozing out of windows as an aimless light smoke. The variety of food also changes at night and so snack types are not so common as wholesome rice, dal, chapatis and parathas. What we find incredible about street food is that there is no class distinction, and so the man standing next to us enjoying a drink of freshly squeezed cane sugar may be so poor that he cannot afford a roof over his head. And so we share this drink and chat. Recognising his plight, we offer to pay for his drink and he embarrassingly accepts and says: 'God bless and may you be blessed with good health and prosperity!'

It is not possible to talk about street food without describing the people on the street, who are never shy to talk and help you out. They love the energy of the street like you do and want to be a part of it; the street children; the street vendors; the rickshaw pullers; the shoppers; a street family sleeping under a newly constructed bridge; and of course good wholesome street food.

We walk past a lady squatting on a mat who is finishing off the most wonderful henna decoration on the hands and arms of a lady customer. She requests our custom many times saying that she will just decorate one hand, and we say 'sorry, no time today'. Disappointed not to tattoo us with henna, she pulls out a business card and points out her mobile number; she says 'call me, when you have more time... I'll give you lovely girls a good discount!'

There are now famous street food joints where a prime minister or a maharaja visited and enjoyed a tandoori chicken. These enigmatic people's photographs will be visible somewhere on a wall, totally out of place for a smoky open-front road-side restaurant. No doubt the photograph frame has a lopsided corner, which bothers us to a great extent, but doesn't worry anyone else around – it's been there for some 40 odd years. Some street food vendors have been plying their trade for many generations; starting off with a small cart over 50 years ago and then finally being able to acquire a corner on the street. They will be able to tell you how a certain recipe popular in Pakistan came into being on the streets of Delhi; how they brought it with them when they came to Delhi just as India and Pakistan was being formed.

The streets are so vibrant with noise and commotion that your ears will beg for silence. This wish can never be answered even at night – the long haul drivers pull in at the street *dhabbas* (similar to traveller's inns many years back) and demand freshly cooked tandoori roti with chicken and sometimes a *charpai* (a rope strung bed on a wooden frame) to rest themselves for a few hours. It is said that Mumbai never sleeps – the industrialist, factory workers, trains, totting cars and Bollywood stars run all day and night. Nothing changes on the street except the street people and changes in menu.

We promise our readers that this book is going to be even more popular than the first as all our efforts have been on keeping cooking to a minimum time limit without any loss of food value, whilst introducing a new range of spices. We have prioritised taste and so the street foods of India are being introduced. We hope you will enjoy cooking with fresh and fast ideas!

# Tez aur Aasaan!

## How to be Quick and Easy!

Quick and easy cooking does not mean that food must come out of tins, jars and packets or be dehydrated; nevertheless, these convenience foods can be used in conjunction with fresh fruit, vegetables and meats to create delicious, super-speedy meals.

Here are some of our tips for quick and easy cooking:

### 1. Onions to be chopped up and browned

Chop 10–15 medium onions, fry in 3–4 tablespoons oil with a sprinkling of salt (which will help them brown quicker) and keep them in an airtight container in the fridge for a week. You can then always have these on hand for cooking.

### 2. Fresh ingredients on standby

Fill a jar each of freshly chopped garlic and ginger mixed with 1 tablespoon oil. Keep it in the fridge, and use when required. You can also buy it ready-made as a paste from any large supermarket or an Indian grocer. It is also a good idea to dry roast 15–20 g (½–¾ oz) each of cumin and coriander seeds in advance and store them in airtight containers in the freezer for up to 6 months; label them, as they look very similar.

### 3. Coriander leaves

These can be chopped, mixed with a little oil and then frozen in ice-cube trays. Just pop a cube out and use as needed. Fresh coriander leaves can also be kept in a jar with enough water to cover the leaves and a plastic bag over the top and then placed in the fridge. The water should be changed every 2–3 days.

### 4. Buy wisely

Buy bagged fresh spinach pre-washed; good-quality frozen peas and fruits; good-quality unsalted nuts; tinned black beans, kidney beans and/or chickpeas; dried split peas and red lentils; coconut milk; frozen or fresh prawns and meats. Remember that fish and prawns take less time to prepare and so it is excellent to have them pre-skinned and shelled ready for use.

### 5. Boiled rice

So many people struggle cooking rice that is light and fluffy. It is not entirely their fault since newly harvested rice has a higher water content and so requires less water added to it when cooking. Another factor is that larger quantities like 5 cups or more require less water than if cooked in smaller quantities.

Having said all this, it is a matter of testing and getting to know your rice brand. Stick to it and either increase or decrease the water added and use our method of cooking rice as given in our first book. The only other solution we have is to buy a rice cooker or steamer or use boil-in-the-bag or pre-cooked and packaged rice. The drawback when buying boil-in-the-bag or pre-cooked rice is that it can work out a tad expensive when used on a regular basis.

## 6. No need to stock up on specialist Indian equipment

Apart from a *kadhi*, which is similar to a wok but heavier and flatter, or a *tava*, which is similar to a frying pan but with no raised edges, you can get away with general kitchen equipment. Another item, much adored by Indians and very helpful for quick and easy cooking, is the pressure cooker. Depending on the size of the family, you will find many varieties from the 1 litre (1¾ pint) flat-pan type to a large 10 litre (16 pint) size and more. They are extremely handy to have since the time of cooking is reduced by nearly half or more. When cooking dals without an overnight soak, using a pressure cooker is very fast. One more item you may need if you are fond of biryanis, is the *handi*; this is a heavy-based saucepan with a larger base than the top and a lid.

## 7. Buy an electric hand whisk or liquidiser

These are great tools for wet grinding like blitzing together ginger/garlic to make a paste. A pestle and mortar is also handy.

## 8. Have a good set of sharp knives

This is always a bonus when cooking. Make sure that they are either hung up or stored in a wooden casket. Knives stored in a drawer rub with other implements and lose their sharpness.

## 9. Organise your spices and cooking ingredients

Having everything organised and to hand before you start cooking will help reduce the overall preparation and cooking time.

## 10. Get prepared in advance

Read a recipe in full and see how much you can prepare in advance to save on preparation time when you come to assemble a dish. For example, it is always advisable to soak dals the day before (see page 14) and marinate your meat and fish in advance wherever possible to drastically cut down your cooking time. As mentioned already, have certain fresh ingredients ready chopped in the fridge, too.

# How to be Quick and Easy!

## Saving time

You can store dals (lentils) that have been soaked and/or boiled, which then only need a final touch. This reduces time in washing, soaking and cooking when you come to make the full recipe. Fully cooked dals can also be stored in the freezer and boiled up again with some water; add fresh coriander and some chopped onions to garnish. We generally, have a couple of dals washed and soaking in water in containers ready to go kept in the fridge. If the dal is not used then, within a few days, it is transferred to the freezer for future use.

## Storing in the fridge and freezer

Many people have said that meat curries taste better after a day in the fridge – well, we feel that the spices tone down after several hours and don't taste as sharp. If you like it this way then, just go ahead with cooking a larger portion and then have some the next day as well.

Kebabs are great to make up in large batches, freeze uncooked kebabs and then they are ready to be pulled out whenever you like. They are the handiest things to have frozen up especially when friends and relatives pop in for a meal or a drink.

One of our friends always had 4–5 boiled and skinned potatoes in her fridge, and out of curiosity we asked her why she did this. Well, as it turns out, they seem to be required in many of our recipes and there is no wasting time in this activity when they are already prepped and in the fridge.

Homemade paneer cheese (see opposite page) can also be made up in a large batch and then stored in small portions in the freezer ready to be used. You can cut them up into the appropriate size and store them in small zip-lock bags. Alternatively, you could fry them up before freezing.

## Useful ingredients

### For your storecupboard

basmati rice
plain flour
wholewheat (atta) flour
gram flour
salt and black pepper
sodium bicarbonate
sugar
chickpeas
red kidney beans
mung dal beans
red split lentils
black beans
tinned pulses
tomato purée
tinned chopped plum
  tomatoes
coconut milk
desiccated coconut
dried mint
ground nutmeg
ground cinnamon
dried red chillies
stock cubes

oil (we favour rapeseed oil, but any oil can be used)

### For your fridge/freezer

butter
eggs
natural yogurt
Greek yogurt
fresh coriander
chicken fillets
diced lamb
lamb mince
mixed frozen vegetables
tamarind paste

### For your vegetable basket

potatoes
onions
garlic
chillies
ginger
tomatoes
lemons
limes

## The spice spoon

You will notice that every recipe in this book measures spices either by a teaspoon or spice spoon. A spice spoon is a specially made spoon sold with our ready-made spice boxes. If you do not have one, remember that 1 spice spoon is equivalent to ½ teaspoon.

# Essential Recipes

## Making a ginger–garlic paste

100 g (3½ oz) garlic cloves, peeled
100 g (3½ oz) ginger, peeled and chopped
1–2 teaspoons oil

Blitz all the ingredients in a blender to a smooth paste, adding more oil if necessary. Pour into an airtight container and store in the fridge for up to 4 weeks.

Use 2 teaspoons in a recipe that serves 4 people. To store in the freezer, place 2 teaspoon quantities into ice-cube tray compartments and freeze until required.

## Making paneer cheese

Paneer is readily available in most supermarkets but if you do have time, it's easy to make your own. Just follow the recipe below, which makes approximately 200–250 g (7–8 oz) paneer.

2 litres (3½ pints) whole milk
Juice of 2 lemons, strained

Line a colander with muslin or a thin cotton cloth. Bring the milk to the boil in a heavy-based saucepan over medium–high heat. When the milk is fully boiled, reduce the heat, stirring occasionally, to prevent sticking to the bottom of the saucepan.

Pour the lemon juice onto the surface of the milk in a steady stream and stir continuously. Stir gently when the milk begins to show signs of curdling and clumping at the surface. You should have a large white mass of curdled milk (the paneer) on top of a yellow-green liquid (the whey). If not, then add some more lemon juice and gently stir.

Strain into the muslin-lined colander and discard the whey. Tie the ends of the muslin loosely above the paneer. Run it under cold water for a few minutes and then, wearing rubber gloves, squeeze the muslin tightly to remove any remaining whey and form into a ball. Hang the paneer by the top ends of the muslin cloth (over a bowl) for an hour to drain as much of the whey as possible. Remove the paneer from the muslin and place on a board, cutting it to the desired size before using.

# Essential Recipes

## Chaat Masala
### Chaat Masala Spice Mix

¼ teaspoon whole black peppercorns
½ teaspoon salt

**FROM YOUR SPICE BOX**

**WHOLE SPICES**

½ teaspoon (1 spice spoon) cumin seeds
2 teaspoons (4 spice spoons) coriander seeds
1 clove
2.5-cm (1-inch) cinnamon stick

**GROUND SPICES**

½ teaspoon (1 spice spoon) black rock salt
3 teaspoons (6 spice spoons) mango powder
½ teaspoon (1 spice spoon) chilli
¼ teaspoon (½ spice spoon) ginger

*MAKES 50 g (2 oz) OF CHAAT MASALA*

Dry roast the cumin seeds from the whole spices in a hot frying pan over medium heat for 1 minute or until dark brown. Transfer to a pestle and mortar and grind to a fine powder. Set aside.

Dry roast the rest of the whole spices in the hot frying pan for 1 minute. Transfer to a pestle and mortar and grind to a powder.

Add the peppercorns, salt, rock salt, ground roasted cumin, mango powder, ground chilli and ginger. Grind for 2 minutes to mix together until a fine powder forms.

Transfer to an airtight container and use when required. Use within 2–3 months.

## Imli Chutney
### Tamarind Chutney

300 g (10 oz) tamarind
500 ml (16 fl oz) boiling water
1½ tablespoons light olive oil
¼ teaspoon salt
6 tablespoons dark brown muscovado sugar

**FROM YOUR SPICE BOX**

**WHOLE SPICE**

½ teaspoon (1 spice spoon) cumin seeds

**GROUND SPICE**

½ teaspoon (1 spice spoon) chilli

*SERVES 4*

Soak the tamarind in the boiling water, breaking the pulp down with the back of a spoon. Leave for about 10–15 minutes.

Push the tamarind through a sieve into a clean bowl, to remove the pulp and juice. Set aside.

Heat a small frying pan over medium heat and dry roast the cumin seeds for 1 minute or until dark brown. When cool, transfer to a pestle and mortar and grind to a fine powder.

Heat the oil in a heavy-based saucepan over medium heat and add the ground roasted cumin and the chilli with all the rest of the ingredients.

Stir well and cook for 6–8 minutes, stirring occasionally. Leave to cool. Store in an airtight container in the fridge for 4–6 days.

Serve with Potato Chaat (see page 32) if liked.

## Dhania Chutney
## Coriander Chutney

2 teaspoons olive oil
60 g (2½ oz) fresh coriander, plus extra to garnish
1 green chilli, deseeded and cut in half
¼ teaspoon salt (or to taste)
3 tablespoons Greek-style yogurt

**FROM YOUR SPICE BOX**
**WHOLE SPICE**
½ teaspoon (1 spice spoon) mustard seeds

*SERVES 6*

Heat the oil in a small frying pan over medium–high heat and add the mustard seeds. When the seeds begin to sizzle, remove from the heat and set aside.

Put the coriander, green chilli, salt and 1 tablespoon of the yogurt in a food processor or blender and blitz until smooth.

Add the fried mustard seeds and the remaining yogurt to the paste and blend for a further 3 seconds.

Garnish with coriander leaves and serve chilled with starters or as an accompaniment to a main meal.

## Pudina-Dahi Chutney
## Mint and Yogurt Chutney

25 g (1 oz) fresh mint leaves, plus extra to garnish
250 ml (8 fl oz) Greek-style yogurt
½ green chilli, deseeded and chopped
Salt

*SERVES 4*

Put all of the ingredients in a food processor or blender and blitz until smooth. Pour into a serving dish and garnish with mint leaves. Serve immediately.

# Masala Dabba The Spice Box

This Indian spice box will be your right-hand tool when creating the recipes in this book or any kind of Indian cooking. Use the spices below to create your very own masala dabba or buy a ready-made Flavours & Spices one that holds all of the spices you need to cook any of the recipes in this book. Our original spice box contained 13 spices:

Chilli

Coriander

Cumin seeds

Ground cumin

Fennel

Ginger

Turmeric

Cinnamon; Bay leaf

Cardamom

Cloves

Mustard seeds

Garam masala

## NEW SPICES ADDED

You can now feel more experimental with your cooking as we have added five more spices to accommodate a larger range in Indian cooking:

Mango powder

Asafoetida

Coriander seeds

Curry leaves

Black rock salt

## OTHER SPICES USED

These 3 spices are worth buying if you do a lot of Indian cooking.

Star anise

Fenugreek leaves

Dried red chillies

These flavours we wish to introduce to you are essential when looking into a larger range of Indian cooking. In this book we have restricted our ingredient lists to what would normally be available to you in your storecupboard or things that you could easily shop for locally. This is how we decide on our family menu everyday; see what fresh ingredients are in the fridge and storecupboard, then find a recipe and simply cook. Once the spices are within your reach, you will easily be able to turn a plain old cabbage or cauliflower or some chicken breasts into a delicious meal!

*Aalp-aahaar*

Little Snacks and Starters

# Namkeen

## Bombay-style Snack Mix

2 tablespoons oil

75 g (3 oz) roasted and unsalted peanuts, shelled

75 g (3 oz) raw cashew nuts

75 g (3 oz) raw or blanched almonds

3 garlic cloves, chopped

1 teaspoon sesame seeds

50 g (2 oz) cornflakes

50 g (2 oz) puffed rice cereal

6 dried apricots, finely diced

½ teaspoon caster sugar

¼–½ teaspoon salt

**FROM YOUR SPICE BOX**

**WHOLE SPICES**

½ teaspoon (1 spice spoon) mustard seeds

½ teaspoon (1 spice spoon) cumin seeds

10 small curry leaves

**GROUND SPICES**

½ teaspoon (1 spice spoon) chilli

½ teaspoon (1 spice spoon) turmeric

¼ teaspoon (½ spice spoon) ginger

½ teaspoon (1 spice spoon) mango powder

*SERVES 4*

Heat half the oil in a shallow saucepan over medium heat. Add all the raw nuts and fry for 1–2 minutes until light brown in colour, stirring frequently. Remove the nuts from the oil with a slotted spoon and place on kitchen paper to drain. Set aside.

Add the remaining oil and the mustard seeds from the whole spices to the hot pan and fry for about 30 seconds until they begin to pop. Add the rest of the whole spices as well as the garlic and cook for another 20–30 seconds.

Remove the pan from heat and then add the chilli, turmeric and ginger from the ground spices as well as the sesame seeds. Stir well to mix the spices into the oil.

Add the cornflakes, puffed rice cereal and the nuts to the pan turning the mixture gently until everything is well mixed and coated with the spice oil. Turn the spiced mixture into a large bowl and add the apricots.

Sprinkle sugar, salt and the mango powder from the ground spices over the cereal. Mix the mixture well before leaving to cool completely. Store in an airtight container for up to 2–3 weeks and serve as a snack with drinks before a meal.

*A savoury snack that is relished in every home.*

# Sukha Mirchi Phaal

## Chilli Nuts

½ teaspoon freshly ground
   black pepper
½ teaspoon salt
1 teaspoon oil
1 teaspoon butter
350 g (11½ oz) mixed nuts
   (unsalted cashew nuts,
   almonds with skins on
   or blanched, roasted and
   unsalted peanuts, shelled with
   no skin)

**FROM YOUR SPICE BOX**
**GROUND SPICES**
1 teaspoon (2 spice spoons)
   chilli
¼ teaspoon (½ spice spoon)
   cumin
½ teaspoon (1 spice spoon)
   mango powder

*SERVES 4–6*

Mix together the black pepper and salt with the chilli, cumin and mango powder from the ground spices in a small bowl. Set aside.

Heat the oil and butter together in a heavy-based saucepan over medium heat. When hot, add the nuts and brown for 3–5 minutes, stirring continuously to prevent burning. Remove the nuts with a slotted spoon and drain on kitchen paper.

While still hot, put all the nuts into the bowl with the spice mixture and stir well so that the nuts are well coated with the spices.

When cold, store in an airtight container for up to 2 weeks. Serve cold with hot or cold drinks.

# Paneer–Dahi Raita

## Paneer Yogurt Dip

250 ml (8 fl oz) natural yogurt

100 g (3½ oz) Homemade Paneer (see page 15), crumbled

¼ small red onion, finely chopped

1 small tomato, finely chopped

1 tablespoon freshly chopped coriander leaves, to finish (optional)

Salt, to taste

**FROM YOUR SPICE BOX**

**WHOLE SPICE**

¼ teaspoon (½ spice spoon) cumin seeds

**GROUND SPICE**

A pinch of (¼ spice spoon) chilli

*SERVES 4–6*

Dry roast the cumin seeds from the whole spices in a hot frying pan over low heat for about 1 minute or until dark brown. Transfer to a pestle and mortar and grind to a fine powder. Add the ground chilli and set aside.

In a bowl, whisk the yogurt and a pinch of salt together until smooth. Add the crumbled paneer and blend with a whisk for 30 seconds, making sure to leave some crumbled paneer visible. Add the rest of the ingredients and mix gently to combine.

Spoon into a serving bowl and sprinkle with the cumin-chilli mixture and the coriander (if using). Serve cold with any spicy meal or as a dip on its own with crackers.

**Time-saving Tip:**
• You could use shop-bought paneer instead of homemade, but soak it in hot water for 10 minutes first to soften.

*Priya's lovely niece manages to whiz this creamy paneer dip up in minutes, but it never reaches the dining table – as her niece always finishes it while chatting to her!*

# Moongphali Pakora
## Nut Pakora

200 g (7 oz) gram (chickpea)
   flour
1 teaspoon lemon juice
½ teaspoon carom seeds
   (optional)
1 tablespoon freshly chopped
   coriander leaves
1 teaspoon salt
½ teaspoon freshly ground
   black pepper
175–200 ml (6–7 fl oz) water
160 g (5½ oz) roasted and
   unsalted peanuts, shelled
Oil, for deep-frying
Natural yogurt with a little
   freshly chopped coriander
   or mint, mixed in, or Mint
   and Yogurt Chutney (see
   page 17), to serve

**FROM YOUR SPICE BOX**
**GROUND SPICE**
½ teaspoon (1 spice spoon)
   chilli

*SERVES 4–6*

Mix the gram flour, lemon juice, carom seeds (if using), fresh coriander, salt and pepper together in a large bowl along with the ground chilli. Add the water and mix to make a thick smooth batter. Add the peanuts and mix well.

Heat the oil in a heavy-based deep frying pan over medium heat. Divide the batter roughly into 2 batches and then drop teaspoonfuls of the batter mixture from one batch into the oil. Turn the batter balls regularly with a slotted spoon to prevent burning on one side.

Remove the pakoras with a slotted spoon after 2–3 minutes when they are deep golden brown and drain on kitchen paper.

Add the second batch of batter balls, a teaspoonful at a time, while the oil is still hot, but lower the heat if it starts smoking at any point. Leave the pakoras to cool before serving. Serve with a herbed yogurt or the mint and yogurt chutney for dipping and with hot or cold drinks.

**Variations:**
• You could use lightly salted nuts as long as you reduce the amount of salt used.
• You can also make smaller balls with 1–2 nuts in each.

# Til Murgh Tikka

## Sesame Chicken Bites

150 ml (¼ pint) water

2 skinless and boneless chicken breasts, cut into large bite-sized pieces

2 tablespoons butter

2.5-cm (1-inch) piece of fresh ginger, roughly chopped

3 garlic cloves

1 onion

1 green chilli, deseeded

1 egg, beaten

½ teaspoon salt

½ teaspoon freshly ground black pepper

3 tablespoons freshly chopped coriander leaves

7–8 tablespoons sesame seeds

Oil, for shallow frying

Lime wedges and chutney, to serve

**FROM YOUR SPICE BOX**

**WHOLE SPICES**

1 teaspoon (2 spice spoons) cumin seeds

2 teaspoons (4 spice spoons) coriander seeds

**GROUND SPICES**

¾ teaspoon (1½ spice spoons) chilli

1 teaspoon (2 spice spoons) ginger

1 teaspoon (2 spice spoons) mango powder

*MAKES 14*

*When we could smell roasting spices floating down the street on our way home from school, we knew we were in for a treat!*

Dry roast the cumin and coriander seeds from the whole spices in a hot frying pan over low heat for about 1 minute until dark brown. Transfer to a pestle and mortar and grind to a fine powder. Set aside.

Boil the water in a saucepan, add the chicken pieces and cook for about 10–15 minutes until tender. Boil to reduce all the water. Add the butter and stir the chicken pieces several times so that they are well coated in the melting butter. Transfer to a bowl and finely shred the chicken pieces.

Put the ginger, garlic, onion and green chilli in a food processor or blender and blitz to a purée. Pour this mixture over the chicken.

Add all the dry roasted ground spices, the egg, salt, pepper and coriander leaves to the chicken. Mix all the ingredients well with the spices and chicken so that the chicken is well coated. Transfer to the fridge for 10 minutes to chill.

Take a small amount of the chilled mixture and make a small ball the size of an apricot. Press the ball gently to flatten (tikka).

Spread the sesame seeds out in a shallow dish and add the tikka, one by one, turning and pressing gently to cover the tikka with sesame seeds all over. Keep the tikka pieces on a plate ready to be fried.

Heat the oil in a frying pan or flat griddle pan over medium heat. When hot, place all the tikkas in the pan and cook them gently for 2 minutes on each side, turning carefully with a spatula, until golden in colour. Serve as a snack or starter with lime wedges and a chutney of your choice.

**Note:**
• If you feel that the tikka are going to be fragile and not hold together well, add 2–3 tablespoons of fresh white breadcrumbs to the mix before you mould into tikka shapes.

# Aloo Chaat

## Potato Chaat

3 potatoes

1 tablespoon oil

1 tablespoon freshly chopped
coriander leaves

1 teaspoon Tamarind and Mint
Chutney (see page 134)

1 teaspoon Mint and Yogurt
Chutney (see page 17)

1 tablespoon Bombay mix
(optional)

Salt, to taste

**FROM YOUR SPICE BOX**

**WHOLE SPICE**

½ teaspoon (1 spice spoon)
cumin seeds

**GROUND SPICES**

1 teaspoon (2 spice spoons)
Chaat Masala (see page 16)

½–1 teaspoon (1–2 spice
spoons) chilli

*SERVES 4*

Dry roast the cumin seeds from the whole spices in a hot frying pan over low heat for about 1 minute or until dark brown. Transfer to a pestle and mortar and grind to a fine powder. Set aside.

Cook the unpeeled potatoes in a saucepan of boiling water and when fork soft, drain and leave to cool. When cool, peel the skins and cut the potatoes into cubes.

Heat the oil in a frying pan over medium heat. When hot, fry the potatoes for 10 minutes until brown. Remove with a slotted spoon and place in a bowl.

Add the Chaat Masala, the chilli from the ground spices, roasted cumin seeds and the coriander leaves to the bowl and toss together a few times.

Add the tamarind and mint chutney, mint and yogurt chutney, salt to taste, more ground chilli (for a spicier taste) and mix well.

Sprinkle the Bombay mix over the potato chaat when you are ready to serve (if using) to give the chaat a crunchy texture. Serve hot as a snack.

**Variation:**
• Substitute the chutneys with a squeeze of lemon juice and mix well.

**Time-saving Tip:**
• To make the cooking quicker, dry roast coriander and cumin seeds and keep them in airtight containers until ready to use. They will keep for several months.

*When Mum had a day of religious fasting, she could only eat fried potatoes at the end of her fasting period – we liked to join her in this fast with aloo chaat!*

# Shami Kababs

## Lamb Patties

100 g (3½ oz) chana dal, washed and then soaked in boiled salted water for 10 minutes

2 tablespoons oil, plus extra for greasing

1 large red onion, chopped

1 tablespoon Ginger-garlic Paste (see page 15)

1–2 green chillies, deseeded and finely chopped

3 tablespoons freshly chopped mint leaves

800 g (1 lb 10 oz) boneless lamb, chopped roughly into very small pieces

3 tablespoons freshly chopped coriander leaves

1 tablespoon lemon juice

1 egg

2-3 tablespoons fresh white breadcrumbs

Oil, for shallow frying

Salt

Lemon wedges, to serve

*Lamb patties can be made in large quantities and frozen before cooking. Lay the patties between sheets of greaseproof paper when freezing to keep them separate. When ready to use, defrost and then fry as from the final step.*

**FROM YOUR SPICE BOX**

**WHOLE SPICE**

½ teaspoon (1 spice spoon) cumin seeds

**GROUND SPICES**

½ teaspoon (1 spice spoon) chilli

½ teaspoon (1 spice spoon) turmeric

½ teaspoon (1 spice spoon) garam masala

*MAKES 12*

Boil the chana dal in their soaking water for 15–20 minutes, until they are soft but still retain their shape (al dente). Drain and set aside.

Meanwhile, heat the oil in a large lidded saucepan over medium heat. Add the cumin seeds and fry for about 30 seconds until they begin to sizzle. Add the onion and some salt to taste. Cook for 3–5 minutes until browned.

Add the ginger-garlic paste and all the ground spices to the onions. Cook for 1 minute, stirring and then add the green chillies, mint and lamb pieces.

Stir the meat in the spices so that it is well coated. Cover the pan with foil and then seal with the lid. Simmer for 25 minutes, stirring occasionally, until the meat is tender. If required, add 100–150 ml (3½–5 fl oz) or more water if it starts to look too dry.

When the meat is tender, boil and reduce the water as much as possible and then add the chana dal and fresh coriander. Check the salt and add more if needed. Mix well. Remove from heat, stir in the lemon juice and then leave to cool.

Transfer the contents of the saucepan to a food processor or blender, add the egg and breadcrumbs and blitz together to form a dough mixture – don't over-process, the meat should retain a fibrous and thread-like consistency. Put the mixture in a bowl and chill in the fridge for at least 15 minutes.

Grease your hands with a little oil and divide the meat dough into 12 equal-sized portions. Roll each portion into a ball and gently press to flatten into thick shaped disks between your palms.

Heat the oil in a frying pan over medium heat and fry all the lamb patties for 2–3 minutes on each side until browned. Serve these as a snack with lemon wedges, a chutney of your choice or as part of a salad.

# Paneer Chaat

## Shallow-fried Paneer Chaat

2 tablespoons oil

250 g (8 oz) Homemade Paneer (see page 15) or shop-bought, cut into bite-sized pieces

A few freshly chopped coriander leaves, to finish

Salt

**FROM YOUR SPICE BOX**

**GROUND SPICES**

2 pinches of (¼ spice spoon) Chaat Masala (see page 16)

¼ teaspoon (½ spice spoon) chilli

¼ teaspoon (½ spice spoon) cumin

¼ teaspoon (½ spice spoon) ginger

¼ teaspoon (½ spice spoon) mango powder

*SERVES 4*

Heat the oil in a shallow frying pan over high heat until hot.

Slide the paneer pieces from a plate slowly into the pan. Use a splatter guard if required.

Turn the heat down to medium and fry for 1–2 minutes on each side, turning the paneer carefully with a spatula. When the edges start to brown, transfer with a slotted spoon to a serving plate.

Take pinches of Chaat Masala and each of the ground spices and sprinkle over the paneer pieces. Turn the paneer very carefully so that it is well coated. Finally sprinkle with salt.

Finish with chopped coriander and serve hot as snack.

# Bhuna Huva Maki

## Street Corn-on-the-Cob

4 corn-on-the-cobs
½ teaspoon salt
½ a lime or lemon

**FROM YOUR SPICE BOX**
**GROUND SPICES**
½ teaspoon (1 spice spoon)
  chilli
¼ teaspoon (½ spice spoon)
  black rock salt

*SERVES 4*

Boil the corn-on-the-cobs in a saucepan of boiling water for about 10 minutes until nearly tender.

Preheat the grill to high.

Mix together both the ground spices and some salt in a small bowl.

Cook the corn-on-the-cobs under the hot grill for 10 minutes or until brown and crisp all over according to your taste. Turn the cobs regularly during cooking to cook evenly.

Remove the cobs from the heat. Take the lime half and dip the cut side into the spice mixture.

Rub the lime all over the corn-on-the-cobs, re-dipping the lime in the spice mixture occasionally, making sure all the kernels are coated.

Cut the cobs into pieces (using a steak fork and sharp knife) and pierce them with forks or skewers. Serve immediately, with the lime half cut into wedges.

**Variation:**
• You may wish to vary this recipe by boiling the corn-on-the-cobs and rubbing the spice mixture with a little butter. This is great grilled on a hot barbecue for the authentic taste.

**Time-saving Tip:**
• Use ready-made corn kebabs, pre-packaged with skewers inserted.

*These deliciously spicy corn snacks are generally served hot on the side streets of India. We love eating them freshly roasted by the roadside.*

# Sabudana Khichadi

## Savoury Tapioca

250 g (8 oz) tapioca, washed and soaked overnight

2 tablespoons oil

1 tablespoon butter

2 boiled potatoes, peeled and cut into small cubes

1 green chilli, deseeded and finely chopped

250 g (8 oz) roasted and unsalted peanuts, skinned and crushed

50 ml (2 fl oz) water (optional)

1 tablespoon lemon juice

2 tablespoons freshly chopped coriander leaves

**FROM YOUR SPICE BOX**

**WHOLE SPICES**

½ teaspoon (1 spice spoon) cumin seeds

5 curry leaves

**GROUND SPICE**

½–1 teaspoon (1–2 spice spoons) black rock salt

*SERVES 4–6*

Drain the water from the tapioca and loosen any lumps with a sprinkling of fresh water. Set aside.

Heat the oil and butter in a shallow frying pan over high heat. When hot, add the cumin seeds from the whole spices. When the seeds begin to sizzle, add the curry leaves and cubed potatoes. Fry for about 2 minutes until golden.

Add the soaked tapioca, green chilli and peanuts and fry for a further 2 minutes. Pour in some of the water if required to prevent sticking.

Add the black rock salt and drizzle over the lemon juice. Mix in the coriander leaves and stir all the ingredients in the pan together. Serve immediately.

*A far cry from those soggy tapioca school dinners!*

# Uppma

## Breakfast Semolina

250 g (8 oz) semolina

3 tablespoons oil

20 g (¾ oz) roasted and
  unsalted peanuts, skinned

1 tablespoon chana dal

5-cm (2-inch) piece of fresh
  ginger, chopped

1–2 green chillies, deseeded
  and finely chopped

1 red onion, finely chopped

500 ml (17 fl oz) water

½ teaspoon salt

**TO SERVE**

Lime wedges

Coconut Chutney
  (see page 136)

**FROM YOUR SPICE BOX**

**WHOLE SPICES**

½ teaspoon (1 spice spoon)
  mustard seeds

½ teaspoon (1 spice spoon)
  cumin seeds

5 curry leaves

**GROUND SPICE**

2 pinches of (¼ spice spoon)
  asafoetida

*SERVES 4*

Dry roast the semolina in a hot frying pan over low heat for 5–7 minutes or until lightly golden brown. Set aside.

Heat the oil in a shallow saucepan over medium heat. When hot, add the mustard seeds from the whole spices. When the seeds begin to pop, add the cumin seeds. When the cumin seeds begin to sizzle, add the peanuts and chana dal.

Fry for 1 minute swirling the ingredients in the oil before adding the curry leaves, chopped ginger, green chillies and pinches of asafoetida. Continue to stir the mixture in a swirling action to cook the peanuts well and mix the ingredients.

Add the onion and fry for 1 minute. Add the water and some salt and bring to the boil.

While stirring constantly, add the semolina slowly into the pan. Keep stirring so that no lumps settle and all the water is reduced. Cover with a lid and cook over low heat for 2 minutes. Take the pan off the heat without lifting the lid.

Rest the mixture in the pan for 3–5 minutes before serving. Serve hot with lime wedges and coconut chutney.

**Variation:**
• Add finely diced cooked potatoes with the peanuts and peas after mixing in the semolina.

*Sereena loves to eat this for breakfast, lunch, dinner, snack...*

# Dahi Balla

## Split Black Gram Lentils in Yogurt

100 g (3½ oz) urid dal, hulls
  removed and washed
100 ml (3½ fl oz) boiling water
½ teaspoon salt, plus extra
  to taste
1 teaspoon ginger juice (made
  by grating some fresh ginger
  and squeezing the gratings in
  your hand to produce liquid)
1 tablespoon freshly chopped
  coriander leaves
A pinch of bicarbonate of soda
Oil, for deep-frying
250 ml (8 fl oz) Greek yogurt
1½ tablespoons caster sugar

**TO FINISH**
Fresh coriander leaves
  (optional)
Coriander Chutney (see
  page 17)
Tamarind and Mint Chutney
  (see page 134)
Pomegranate seeds or
  cranberries (optional)
Bombay mix or Sev mix (a type
  of Bombay mix)

**FROM YOUR SPICE BOX**
**WHOLE SPICE**
½ teaspoon (1 spice spoon)
  cumin seeds

**GROUND SPICE**
½ teaspoon (1 spice spoon)
  chilli
¼ teaspoon (½ spice spoon)
  Chaat Masala (see page 16),
  to finish

*SERVES 4*

Place the dal in a bowl with the boiling water and soak for 15 minutes. Drain half the water into a cup (and reserve) and transfer the dal and remaining water to a food processor. Add the cumin seeds, the salt, ginger juice, coriander and bicarbonate of soda and blitz for 2–3 minutes or until a smooth and thick batter forms (as thick as a cake mix). Add small amounts of water reserved in the cup if required to make the batter looser.

Heat the oil in a heavy-based deep frying pan over high heat until hot and then turn the heat down to medium. Wet a teaspoon with water and scoop out heaped teaspoons of batter and drop them into the pan (use another teaspoon to scrape off the thick batter if it does not fall in easily).

Drop in 5–6 teaspoons at a time and, using a slotted spoon, gently turn and bob each ball in the oil until browned for 2–4 minutes. Lower the heat if the oil begins to smoke and increase the heat if the temperature gets too low. Use a slotted spoon to transfer the cooked balls from the oil to a bowl of cold water and leave to soak for 5 minutes.

Gently press each ball between flat palms to squeeze out the excess water and form a thick disc. Arrange the discs in a shallow plate or bowl and set aside.

Whisk the yogurt, sugar and some salt to taste in a bowl for 1 minute or until smooth. Pour half of the yogurt mixture over the discs to cover them (keep the rest of the yogurt mix in the fridge) and cover the bowl with clingfilm or foil. Transfer to the fridge to keep cool.

Before serving, pour the rest of the yogurt mixture over the discs and sprinkle with ground chilli, Chaat Masala and fresh coriander leaves (if using). Put 3–4 discs on each plate and serve with chutneys, pomegranate seeds or cranberries and sev or Bombay mix as preferred.

**Time-saving Tip:**
• This can be frozen once the dal discs have been formed and defrosted and used when needed or they can be kept in the fridge for a few days once the yogurt mix has been poured over – quick and easy and ready to eat.

*This is one of the most refreshing street foods – Alexa's favourite.*

# Safed Gajar ka Shorba
## Spicy Parsnip Soup

1½ tablespoons oil

1 tablespoon butter

1 onion, chopped

2.5-cm (1-inch) piece of fresh ginger, grated

3 garlic cloves, crushed

500 g (1 lb) parsnips, peeled and grated

800 ml (1⅓ pints) vegetable stock

100 ml (3½ fl oz) milk

50 ml (2 fl oz) single cream

A squeeze of lemon juice

2 tablespoons freshly chopped coriander or parsley leaves

Salt and freshly ground black pepper

**FROM YOUR SPICE BOX**

**GROUND SPICES**

½ teaspoon (1 spice spoon) turmeric

A pinch of (¼ spice spoon) chilli

A pinch of (¼ spice spoon) cumin

*SERVES 4*

Melt the oil and butter in a saucepan over medium heat. When hot, add the onions and fry for about 5 minutes until they are soft and translucent.

Add the ginger, garlic and all the ground spices. Stir to combine all the ingredients with the spices for 1 minute before adding the parsnips and vegetable stock. Cover and simmer for 10 minutes or until the parsnips are tender. Take off the heat.

Transfer the mixture to a food processor or blender (or use a hand-held blender), add the milk and then blitz for a few minutes until smooth.

Return the soup to the pan and put it back over medium heat. Pour in the cream and slowly bring to the boil.

Season with salt and then add the lemon juice, a grind of black pepper and either coriander or parsley leaves.

**Variation:**
• Sometimes when there are no fresh leaves for garnishing, we just dry roast a pinch (¼ spice spoon) of cumin seeds, grind them in a pestle and mortar and then sprinkle on top before serving.

**Time-saving Tip:**
• This soup can be frozen in batches – great for quick lunches.

*The vibrant colour of this soup always brings a smile to Alexa's face.*

# Murgh aur Chaney ka Shorba

## Chicken and Chickpea Soup

1½ tablespoons oil

300 g (10 oz) skinless and boneless chicken breast, cut into very small pieces

1 onion, finely chopped

2 garlic cloves, crushed

2.5-cm (1-inch) piece of fresh ginger, grated

2 carrots, peeled and finely diced

2 potatoes, peeled and diced

100 g (3½ oz) cauliflower, cut into very small florets

1 litre (1¾ pints) chicken stock (made from 2 stock cubes)

1 tablespoon milk

1 x 400 g (13 oz) tin chickpeas, drained and rinsed

2 tomatoes, peeled and diced

1 green chilli, deseeded and finely chopped

A pinch of freshly ground black pepper

¼ green pepper, deseeded and cut into thin strips

2 tablespoons freshly chopped coriander leaves

2 teaspoons lemon juice

1 tablespoon melted ghee or butter

**FROM YOUR SPICE BOX**

**WHOLE SPICE**

¼ teaspoon (½ spice spoon) cumin seeds

*SERVES 4*

Dry roast the cumin seeds in a hot frying pan over low heat for 1 minute or until dark brown. Transfer to a pestle and mortar and grind to a fine powder. Set aside.

Heat the oil in a saucepan over medium heat. When hot, add the chicken and cook for 2–3 minutes. Add the onion, garlic, ginger, carrots, potatoes and cauliflower.

Fry for 5 minutes and then add in the chicken stock and milk, partially cover and cook for 20–25 minutes, stirring occasionally or until the chicken is tender and the vegetables are soft.

After 20 minutes add the chickpeas. Remove from the heat and transfer half the vegetables and chicken with 100 ml (3½ fl oz) of the liquid to a food processor or blender and blitz until smooth. Pour this back into the saucepan and return to medium heat.

Mix in the tomatoes, green chilli, black pepper, green pepper, coriander and lemon juice and stir to combine. Mix in the dry roasted cumin powder and cook for a further 5 minutes.

Heat the ghee or butter and pour this over the soup. Serve hot with naan or crispy bread rolls.

**Time-saving Tip:**
• This can also be frozen in batches.

*Mum's medicine! Delicious, wholesome soup, which always made us feel better.*

# Murgh

Chicken

# Dhaba Murgh
## Street Chicken

2 tablespoons oil

1 large red onion, chopped

2.5-cm (1-inch) piece of fresh ginger, roughly chopped

5 garlic cloves, roughly chopped

3 tomatoes, quartered

2 tablespoons tomato purée

200 g (7 oz) tinned chopped tomatoes

1 green chilli, deseeded and cut in half

¼ teaspoon salt

¼ teaspoon freshly ground black pepper

¼ teaspoon ground cinnamon

500 ml (17 fl oz) water

2 tablespoons ghee or butter

500 g (1 lb) skinless and boneless chicken breasts, cut into bite-sized pieces

1 tablespoon freshly chopped coriander leaves, to finish

**FROM YOUR SPICE BOX**

**WHOLE SPICES**

½ teaspoon (1 spice spoon) cumin seeds

2 cardamoms, pods removed and seeds finely ground

2.5-cm (1-inch) cinnamon stick

3 cloves, ground

**GROUND SPICES**

1 teaspoon (2 spice spoons) chilli

1 teaspoon (2 spice spoons) coriander

½ teaspoon (1 spice spoon) ginger

½ teaspoon (1 spice spoon) turmeric

1 teaspoon (2 spice spoons) mango powder

½ teaspoon (1 spice spoon) garam masala

¼ teaspoon (½ spice spoon) cumin

*SERVES 4*

Heat 1 tablespoon of the oil in a heavy-based saucepan over medium heat. When hot, add the onion and fry for 3–5 minutes until soft and translucent. Add the ginger and garlic and fry for another minute. Take the pan off the heat and leave to cool.

Put the tomatoes, tomato purée, tinned tomatoes, green chilli, salt, pepper, ground cinnamon, the onion mixture, 100 ml (3½ fl oz) of the water with all the ground spices in a food processor or blender and blitz to a smooth paste. Set aside.

Heat the remaining oil and the ghee or butter in a heavy–based saucepan over medium heat. Add the cumin seeds, ground cardamom seeds, cinnamon stick and the ground cloves from the whole spices and fry for 30 seconds. Add the chicken pieces and 100 ml (3½ fl oz) of the water. Cover and cook the chicken stirring occasionally for 10–12 minutes. Remove the lid and boil to reduce the water if any remains and cook the chicken until it is golden brown.

Add the puréed mixture and cook for 15 minutes, stirring every now and then. Add the remaining water and cook for a further 8 minutes over low heat. Finish with a sprinkling of fresh coriander leaves and serve with rice.

**Time-saving Tip:**
• This can be frozen and then defrosted and reheated as needed saving valuable time on a busy night.

*We always look forward to travelling on the national highways in India just to relish dhaba chicken and tandoori naan! There are literally millions of dhabas dotted around the roadsides of India serving dhaba food.*

# Rajasthani Murgh Laccha
## Rajasthani Chicken Strips

500 g (1 lb) skinless and
boneless chicken breast, cut
into strips

4 tablespoons oil

2 large red onions, finely
chopped

1 tablespoon Ginger-garlic
paste (see page 15)

125 ml (4 fl oz) natural yogurt

10 g (¼ oz) ground almonds

1 tablespoon fresh or
desiccated coconut (see Note)

200 ml (7 fl oz) chicken stock

A pinch of freshly ground
black pepper

2 green chillies, deseeded and
finely sliced

1 tablespoon freshly chopped
coriander leaves

Salt

**FROM YOUR SPICE BOX**

**WHOLE SPICES**

½ teaspoon (1 spice spoon)
cumin seeds

2 cardamoms, pods removed
and seeds finely ground

**GROUND SPICES**

2 teaspoons (4 spice spoons)
chilli

2 teaspoons (4 spice spoons)
coriander

½ teaspoon (1 spice spoon)
ginger

*SERVES 4*

Put the chicken in a heavy-based saucepan over medium heat and cover
with a lid. Steam the chicken in its own water for 5 minutes and then
set aside.

Heat the oil in a heavy-based saucepan over medium heat. When hot,
add the cumin seeds from the whole spices. When they begin to sizzle,
add the onions and fry for 5 minutes until they are soft.

Add the ginger-garlic paste and fry for 2–3 minutes. Add all the ground
spices as well as some salt to taste. Mix the spices well with the onions
and then take the pan off the heat.

Whisk the yogurt, almonds and coconut in a bowl for 1 minute and then
add it to the spice mixture. Stir well to combine and then pour over the
steamed chicken.

Return the chicken pan to the heat and cook slowly, stirring frequently,
for about 5 minutes until the sauce becomes thick.

Add the chicken stock and black pepper and continue to cook over
medium heat for 15 minutes, until the chicken is tender. Boil to reduce
and thicken the sauce as preferred.

Add the ground cardamom and finish with the green chilli and
coriander. Serve hot with rice or any flatbread and accompany with salad,
chutney or raita.

**Note:**
• Re-hydrate unsweetened dried coconut by soaking it in some coconut
milk or water for 10 minutes before draining and using.

**Time-saving Tip:**
• This dish can be frozen and then defrosted and reheated when needed.

*This dish always brings back memories of our journeys
to Rajasthan.*

# Zeera Murgh
## Cumin Chicken

3 tablespoons oil

¼ teaspoon freshly ground
black pepper

2.5-cm (1-inch) piece of fresh
ginger, grated

2 garlic cloves, crushed

800 g (1 lb 10 oz) skinless
chicken pieces (boneless
breast and thighs cut into
pieces)

3–4 green chillies, 1–2 finely
chopped and 1–2 left whole
and pierced

1 tablespoon butter or ghee

100 ml (3½ fl oz) water

2 tablespoons freshly chopped
coriander leaves, plus extra
to finish

Salt

**FROM YOUR SPICE BOX**

**WHOLE SPICES**

1 teaspoon (2 spice spoons)
coriander seeds

3 teaspoons (6 spice spoons)
cumin seeds

3 cardamoms, pods removed
and seeds finely ground

**GROUND SPICE**

1 teaspoon (2 spice spoons)
garam masala

*SERVES 6*

Dry roast the coriander seeds and half the cumin seeds in a hot frying
pan over high heat for about 30 seconds or until light brown. Transfer to
a pestle and mortar and grind to a fine powder. Set aside.

Dry roast another ½ teaspoon (1 spice spoon) of the cumin seeds.
Transfer to a pestle and mortar and grind to a powder. Mix with the
garam masala in a small bowl and set aside.

Heat the oil in a heavy-based saucepan over medium heat. When hot,
add the ground cardamom seeds, black pepper and the remaining cumin
seeds. Fry for about 30 seconds until the seeds begin to sizzle.

Add the ginger, garlic, roasted coriander and cumin powder and some
salt to taste. Fry for 1 minute and then add the chicken and finely
chopped green chillies.

Stir the chicken in to the ingredients for 2 minutes and then cover and
simmer for 20–25 minutes, stirring occasionally, or until the chicken is
tender and the cooking juices are released.

Add the garam masala and cumin seeds mixture followed by the butter
or ghee and the water and stir to mix. Stir for 1 minute and then add the
coriander leaves and whole green chillies. Cover and leave the ingredients
to infuse for about 5 minutes.

Serve hot, sprinkled with freshly chopped coriander, as a snack or as
a main meal with your choice of rice or flatbreads.

**Time-saving Tips:**
• Cut the chicken into bite-sized pieces to speed up the cooking time.
• If you are really short on time, prepare your roasted spices in advance.
Dry roast some coriander and cumin seeds, grind in a pestle and mortar
and keep stored in an airtight container.
• This dish can also be frozen and then defrosted and reheated as needed.

*The smell of roasted cumin really wakes up the senses.*

# Murgh Tandoori
## Tandoori Chicken

2 teaspoons salt

Juice of 1 lemon

800g (1 lb 10 oz) skinless and boneless chicken breasts and thighs, cut into large chunks, and drumsticks

10 tablespoons Greek yogurt

2 tablespoons Ginger-garlic paste (see page 15)

½ teaspoon fenugreek leaves (optional)

2 tablespoons tomato purée

½ teaspoon freshly ground black pepper

1 tablespoon natural red vegetable or flower colouring (i.e. beetroot powder) (optional)

2 tablespoons oil

1½ tablespoons ghee or butter

1 red onion, sliced into rings

Lemon wedges, to serve

**FROM YOUR SPICE BOX**

**GROUND SPICES**

2 teaspoons (4 spice spoons) chilli

1½ teaspoons (3 spice spoons) cumin

½ teaspoon (1 spice spoon) coriander

½ teaspoon (1 spice spoon) turmeric

½ teaspoon (1 spice spoon) garam masala

½ teaspoon (1 spice spoon) Chaat Masala (see page 16)

*SERVES 6*

Mix half the chilli from the ground spices, 1 teaspoon of the salt and half the lemon juice in a small bowl. Make slashes through to the bone of the chicken in the most fleshy parts of the meat on the drumsticks using a sharp knife. Rub the lemon-spice mixture liberally all over the chicken drumsticks and other chicken pieces, making sure it is pushed into the cuts. Cover and set aside.

Put the yogurt, ginger-garlic paste, fenugreek (if using), tomato purée, ground black pepper, remaining salt, all the remaining ground spices and the red colouring (if using) in a large bowl. Mix well and then pour over the chicken making sure it is all coated with marinade. Pour over the oil to give the chicken a final coat. Cover and transfer to the fridge to marinate for 1–4 hours or overnight.

Preheat the oven to 200°C (400°F), gas mark 6. Line a baking tray with foil and place the marinated chicken pieces on it. Cook in the preheated oven for 30 minutes.

Remove the chicken from the oven and transfer to a plate, leaving any marinade residue on the tray. Heat the ghee or butter and a little extra oil in a frying pan over high heat. Place the chicken in the hot pan and sprinkle with the onion and the Chaat Masala. Cook for 4–5 minutes, turning the onions and chicken pieces over a few times to cook well.

Serve hot (although it can also be eaten cold) with a squeeze of lemon juice. Tandoori chicken is best served with a cucumber and mint salad and naan bread.

**Time-saving Tips:**
• Marinate the chicken the day before to save on preparation time.
• The chicken can be frozen once marinated and then fully defrosted and popped in the oven when needed.
• Use 800–900 g (1 lb 10 oz–1 lb 13 oz) boneless chicken pierced onto skewers to speed up the cooking time and cook on a hot barbecue grill for 15–20 minutes.

*Tandoori chicken is always a winner!*

# Dum Badam Murgh

## Infused Almond Chicken

50 g (2 oz) ground almonds

200 ml (7 fl oz) water

3 tablespoons oil

1 tablespoon butter

1 red onion, finely chopped

1 tablespoon Ginger-garlic
paste (see page 15)

500–600 g (1lb–1 lb 3 oz)
skinless and boneless chicken
breasts, cut into smaller than
bite-sized pieces

½ teaspoon salt, or to taste

½ tablespoon freshly chopped
or dried mint leaves

60 ml (2½ fl oz) single cream
or low-fat alternative

2 green chillies, split open
and deseeded or left
whole and pierced

1–2 drops of rosewater essence

**FROM YOUR SPICE BOX**

**WHOLE SPICES**

1 bay leaf

4-cm (1½-inch) cinnamon
stick

4–5 cardamoms, pods removed
and seeds finely ground

**GROUND SPICES**

1 teaspoon (2 spice spoons)
chilli

½ teaspoon (1 spice spoon)
turmeric

*SERVES 4–6*

Mix the ground almonds with 50 ml (2 fl oz) of the water in a small bowl to make a paste. Set aside.

Heat the oil and butter in a shallow frying pan with a good fitting lid over medium heat. When hot, add the whole spices, fry for 30 seconds and then add the onion. Fry for 3–4 minutes or until tender and then add the ginger-garlic paste.

Add the chicken and fry for 1–2 minutes before adding all the ground spices and the salt. Stir to combine and then add the remaining water. Cook for 5 minutes, stirring occasionally.

Add all the remaining ingredients, stir and then put a layer of foil over the pan. Cover with the lid and turn the heat down to low.

Cook for 12–15 minutes, stirring from time to time, and then check to see if the chicken is tender. If not, add another 100–150 ml (3½–5 fl oz) water and cook for a further 5 minutes.

Serve with rice or chapati and a cucumber salad.

# Naryal-Kaju Murgh
## Cashew and Coconut Chicken

40 g (1½ oz) unsalted roasted
  cashew nuts
25 g (1 oz) fresh coconut,
  grated, or desiccated coconut,
  soaked and drained
300 ml (½ pint) water
2 tablespoons oil
1 red onion, diced
1–1½ tablespoons Ginger-
  garlic paste (see page 15)
¼ teaspoon freshly ground
  black pepper
¼ teaspoon fenugreek leaves
  (optional)
500 g (1 lb) skinless and
  boneless chicken breasts (or
  a mix of boneless breast and
  thighs), cut into bite-sized
  pieces
1 teaspoon butter (optional)
3 green chillies, deseeded
  and chopped (or made
  into a paste)
Salt

**TO FINISH**
10 g (½ oz) unsalted and
  roasted cashew nuts, halved
2–3 tablespoons freshly
  chopped coriander leaves
Coconut Chutney (see page
  136)
Lime wedges

**FROM YOUR SPICE BOX**
**WHOLE SPICES**
½ teaspoon (1 spice spoon)
  coriander seeds
½ teaspoon (1 spice spoon)
  cumin seeds
3–4 curry leaves

**GROUND SPICE**
½ teaspoon (1 spice spoon)
  turmeric

*SERVES 4*

Dry roast the coriander seeds from the whole spices in a hot frying pan over high heat for about 1 minute or until they turn dark brown. Transfer to a pestle and mortar and grind to a fine powder. Set aside.

Put the cashew nuts, coconut and 200 ml (7 fl oz) of the water in a food processor or blender and blitz to a smooth paste. Set aside.

Heat the oil in a heavy-based saucepan over medium heat. When hot, add the cumin seeds. When they begin to sizzle, add the onion and some salt. Fry for 2 minutes or until they are soft.

Add the ginger-garlic paste, black pepper, fenugreek (if using) and the turmeric. Stir all the ingredients together for 1 minute and then add the chicken with the remaining water. Cover and simmer, stirring occasionally, for 15 minutes or until the chicken is tender.

Remove the lid, boil to reduce any liquid and brown the chicken in the oil that has separated from the liquid for 2–3 minutes. Add the dry roasted coriander as well as the cashew and coconut paste and green chillies. Simmer and stir for 1–2 minutes or until a thick sauce forms. Cover and simmer, stirring occasionally, for 10–12 minutes. Mix in the butter (if using).

Transfer to a serving dish and top with roasted cashew halves, coriander leaves and lime wedges to finish. Serve hot with basmati rice, Dry Green Beans (see page 96), naan bread or flatbread and coconut chutney.

**Note:**
Fresh coconut is sometimes difficult to find, so you can use unsweetened desiccated coconut mixed with a little water or coconut milk and left to soak for 10–15 minutes instead.

*A very royal dish with cashew and coconut sauce, which in the past, was only served to Maharajas – today, Maharanis (like Alexa and Sereena) can enjoy it as well!*

*Gosht*

Lamb

# Gosht Boti aur Tamater

## Lamb Loin Chops in Tomatoes

3 tablespoons oil

4 lamb loin chops, weighing a total of 500–600 g (1 lb–1 lb 3 oz)

1 teaspoon caster sugar

450 ml (¾ pint) water

250 g (8 oz) tinned chopped tomatoes

200 ml (7 fl oz) passata

2 green chillies, left whole and pierced

Salt

Finely diced red onion, to finish

**FROM YOUR SPICE BOX**

**WHOLE SPICES**

½ teaspoon (1 spice spoon) cumin seeds

2 cloves

2.5-cm (1-inch) cinnamon stick

**GROUND SPICES**

A pinch of asafoetida

1 teaspoon (2 spice spoons) chilli

1¼ teaspoons (2½ spice spoons) fennel

1 teaspoon (2 spice spoons) ginger

¼ teaspoon (½ spice spoon) garam masala

*SERVES 4*

Heat the oil in a heavy-based saucepan over high heat. When hot, add the cumin seeds from the whole spices and fry for about 30 seconds. When they begin to sizzle, add the cloves and cinnamon stick, and the asafoetida from the ground spices. Stir to combine.

Add the lamb chops and some salt to taste and stir before covering and leaving to cook for 5–7 minutes. Boil and reduce the water so that the chops begin to brown in the oil.

Tilt the pan at an angle just slightly to accumulate all the oil in one spot and add the sugar here. Stir to caramelise the sugar in the oil.

Put the pan flat again and add the chilli, fennel and ginger from the ground spices. Stir and add the water. Cover and simmer for 20 minutes or until the meat is tender, the water has reduced and the oil is visible (you may need to add 50 ml (2 fl oz) water if needed), stirring occasionally.

Add the tomatoes and stir for 3 minutes before adding the passata and the green chillies. Cover and simmer for 5–10 minutes, stirring occasionally.

Mix in the garam masala and finish with the finely diced red onion. Serve hot with plain rice or flatbread.

**Time-saving Tips:**
• Choose small chops and cover with foil when simmering to reduce the cooking time.
• This can be frozen and then fully defrosted and reheated as needed.

# Kushur Rogan Josh

## Kashmiri Lamb Rogan Josh

650 g (1 lb 5 oz) boneless leg
  of lamb, cut into small bite-
  sized pieces
4 tablespoons natural yogurt
1 teaspoon salt
4 tablespoons oil
A pinch of nutmeg
1 star anise (optional)
A pinch of mace
1 teaspoon granulated sugar
1 tablespoon ghee or butter
Natural red vegetable or flower
  food colouring – i.e. beetroot
  powder or flowers as used in
  Kashmir (optional)
2 tablespoons tomato purée
200 ml (7 fl oz) water
¼ teaspoon ground cinnamon

**TO FINISH**
4–5 saffron threads, soaked
  in 1 tablespoon warm milk
  for 5 minutes

**FROM YOUR SPICE BOX**
**WHOLE SPICES**
2 bay leaves
1 cardamom, pod removed and
  seeds finely ground
2.5-cm (1-inch) cinnamon
  stick
3 cloves
½ teaspoon (1 spice spoon)
  cumin seeds

**GROUND SPICES**
A pinch (¼ teaspoon)
  asafoetida
1 teaspoon (2 spice spoons)
  chilli
1 teaspoon (2 spice spoons)
  ginger
1½ teaspoons (3 spice spoons)
  fennel
¼ teaspoon (½ spice spoon)
  cumin
½ teaspoon (1 spice spoon)
  garam masala

*SERVES 4*

Put the lamb in a large bowl and mix in the yogurt, salt and the bay leaves and cardamom from the whole spices. Mix and coat the lamb with the ingredients and set aside for 10–15 minutes.

Heat the oil in a heavy-based saucepan over medium heat. When hot, add the remaining whole spices, the asafoetida from the ground spices, the nutmeg, star anise (if using) and mace. Fry for 30 seconds and then add the lamb mixture.

Turn the lamb in the oil several times and cook for 2 minutes to seal the meat pieces. Cover and simmer the lamb in its own juices, stirring occasionally, for 20–25 minutes or until the lamb is tender and the oil is visible again. Add 50–100 ml (2–3½ fl oz) water if required to make the meat tender.

Make a well in the centre of the lamb and add the sugar with the ghee or butter. Add the natural colouring (if using). Cook, stirring frequently, for 1–2 minutes, allowing the sugar to caramelise and then lower the heat and add the remaining ground spices (except the garam masala) and the tomato purée.

Add 100 ml (3½ fl oz) of the water and mix well. Cook and stir frequently for a further 10 minutes or until the oil separates from the lamb. Add the ground cinnamon and the garam masala, stir and pour in remaining water. Cook for 1–2 minutes.

To finish, drizzle with the saffron milk and serve hot with rice and/or chapati and Baby Spring Greens (see page 110).

**Time-saving Tips:**
• Cover the pan with foil when simmering to reduce the cooking time.
• This recipe is perfect for making ahead, freezing and then fully defrosting and reheating for a dinner party as needed.

*This is an all time favourite of ours; you could call it the basic meat recipe with no onions, ginger or garlic – just lamb and spices in natural yogurt.*

# Kheema aur Aloo

## Lamb Mince and Potatoes

3 tablespoons oil

4 potatoes, peeled and each cut into 4

1 red or white onion, chopped

1 tablespoon Ginger-garlic paste (see page 15)

500 g (1 lb) lean minced lamb

4 tomatoes, peeled and diced or ½ x 400 g (13 oz) tin of plum tomatoes, drained of juice and chopped

250 g (8 oz) passata

400 ml (14 fl oz) water

3 tablespoons freshly chopped coriander leaves

Salt

**FROM YOUR SPICE BOX**

**WHOLE SPICE**

½ teaspoon (1 spice spoon) cumin seeds

**GROUND SPICES**

1 teaspoon (2 spice spoons) chilli

½ teaspoon (1 spice spoon) turmeric

1 teaspoon (2 spice spoons) ginger

1 teaspoon (2 spice spoons) fennel

1½ teaspoons (3 spice spoons) coriander

¼ teaspoon (½ spice spoon) cumin

½ teaspoon (1 spice spoon) garam masala

*SERVES 4–6*

Heat the oil in a heavy-based saucepan over high heat. When hot, add the potatoes. Fry for 4–5 minutes until golden brown, stirring occasionally, and then remove with a slotted spoon. Set aside.

Put the cumin seeds into the pan and when they begin to sizzle add the onions. Fry for 3 minutes or until they are soft. Add the ginger-garlic paste and fry for 1 minute before adding the minced lamb.

Cook, stirring frequently, for 5–6 minutes or until the overall colour in the pan changes from pink-red to mostly brown.

Add all the ground spices, except for the gram masala, and some salt to taste. Stir well for 30 seconds and then add in the tomatoes, passata and the cooked potatoes. Cook, stirring, for 2 minutes.

Add the water, cover and simmer for 15–20 minutes or until the potatoes are tender. Stir in the garam masala and half the coriander leaves. Finish with a sprinkling of fresh coriander and serve with rice or flatbread, raita and vegetables of your choice.

**Time-saving Tips:**

• This can be frozen at the end of step 4, but leave the potatoes out. Add the potatoes once fully defrosted and reheated and then continue from step 5.

• If using the tinned plum tomatoes, use some of the drained juice instead of the water.

*For Priya, mince and potatoes was her star 'student meal' as it was so easy to cook. She would have this at least twice a week varying it with mushrooms, peas or colourful peppers.*

# Tandoori Gosht

## Tandoori Lamb Skewers

2 tablespoons oil

1 red onion, minced

5 garlic cloves, crushed

4–5 green chillies, deseeded
and crushed into a paste

1 tablespoon white poppy
seeds, ground

1 teaspoon ginger juice
(see Note)

1 tablespoon thick Greek
yogurt

1 teaspoon paprika

½ teaspoon salt, or to taste

600 g (1 lb 3 oz) lean lamb, cut
into small cubes

Melted butter, for basting

Finely sliced red onion and
lemon wedges, to serve

**FROM YOUR SPICE BOX**

**GROUND SPICE**

2 teaspoons (4 spice spoons)
garam masala

*SERVES 4*

Put the oil, onion, garlic, chillies, ground poppy seeds, ginger juice, yogurt, paprika, garam masala and some salt in a bowl and mix well.

Put the lamb pieces in a shallow dish large enough to hold them all. Rub the marinade all over the lamb pieces, cover with clingfilm and transfer to the fridge for as long as possible, at least 1 hour.

Thread the marinated lamb pieces onto oiled metal skewers and preheat the grill to medium.

Place the lamb skewers in a single layer on the grill tray and grill for 15–18 minutes, brushing with a little melted butter halfway through cooking. Turn the skewers regularly to brown evenly.

Serve hot with a chutney of your choice and Potato Chaat (see page 32), naan, some finely sliced red onion and lemon wedges to finish.

**Note:**
• To make ginger juice, grate a piece of fresh ginger and squeeze the gratings in your hand to produce some juice.

**Time-saving Tips:**
• Marinate the lamb the night before to reduce preparation time.
• The lamb could also be frozen once marinated and then fully defrosted, placed on skewers and grilled as needed.

*Traditionally, lamb pieces are placed on a skewer and cooked in a tandoor (clay oven) but you may like to put them on a barbecue to get the same results. Great to take in a cool box for a barbecue on the beach or a picnic!*

# Badam Gosht

## Lamb in Almond Sauce

2 tablespoons ground almonds

100 ml (3½ fl oz) water

1 large red onion, roughly chopped

1 tablespoon Ginger-garlic paste (see page 15)

1 green chilli, deseeded

4 tablespoons natural yogurt

1 teaspoon lemon juice

½–1 teaspoon salt

¼ teaspoon freshly ground black pepper

500 g (1 lb) boneless leg of lamb, cut into smaller than bite-sized pieces

3 tablespoons oil

1 star anise (optional)

½ tablespoon ghee or butter

A pinch of ground cinnamon

100 ml (3½ fl oz) passata

1 tablespoon tomato purée

**FROM YOUR SPICE BOX**

**WHOLE SPICES**

½ teaspoon (1 spice spoon) cumin seeds

3 cloves

1 bay leaf

3–4 curry leaves, plus extra to finish

2 cardamoms, pods removed and seeds finely ground

**GROUND SPICES**

A pinch (¼ spice spoon) asafoetida

1 teaspoon (2 spice spoons) chilli

½ teaspoon (1 spice spoon) ginger

¾ teaspoon (1½ spice spoons) fennel

½ teaspoon (1 spice spoon) coriander

¼ teaspoon (½ spice spoon) turmeric

½ teaspoon (1 spice spoon) garam masala

*SERVES 4*

Put the ground almonds and water in a bowl and whisk together for 1 minute or until smooth. Set aside.

Put the onion, ginger-garlic paste, green chilli, yogurt, lemon juice, salt and pepper in a food processor or blender and blitz for 2 minutes to form a smooth paste.

Put the lamb in a shallow dish and brush or spoon the paste all over making sure it is completely coated. Set aside for at least 15 minutes.

Heat the oil in a heavy-based lidded saucepan over medium heat. When hot, add all the whole spices along with the asafoetida from the ground spices and the star anise (if using). Fry for 30 seconds.

Add the marinated lamb mixture. Stir to combine the spices with the lamb for a minute and then remove and leave to cool slightly.

Cover the pan with foil and then seal with the lid. Return the pan to medium heat for 20–25 minutes, or until the lamb is cooked and tender.

Remove the foil and add the ghee or butter, ground cinnamon and all the remaining ground spices, except the garam masala. Stir all the ingredients together and cook for 5–8 minutes.

Add the passata and tomato purée. Cook, stirring occasionally, for about 5 minutes and then add the soaked ground almonds and water. Cook for 2–3 minutes or until a thick sauce forms. Mix in the garam masala and finish with some more curry leaves. Serve with rice and naan.

**Time-saving Tip:**
• Longer marinating periods will result in a shorter cooking time; 4 hours to overnight is preferred.

*This is a naughty treat with thick almond sauce mmm... really you don't need any chutneys or raitas. Just delicious!*

# Macchli aur Jhinga
## Fish and Prawns

# Goan Macchli

## Goan Fish Curry

300 g (10 oz) haddock fillets (or any firm white sustainable fish), skin removed and cut into 6-cm (2½-inch) pieces or equal-sized portions

2 small dried red chillies

3 tablespoons oil, plus extra for shallow frying

1 red onion, very finely chopped

1 tablespoons Ginger-garlic paste (see page 15)

4 ripe tomatoes, peeled and chopped

2 teaspoons tamarind paste

1 x 400 ml (14 fl oz) tin coconut milk

100 ml (3½ fl oz) water

1 teaspoon malt vinegar

1–2 green chillies, left whole and pierced

Salt and freshly ground black pepper

### TO FINISH

A squeeze of lime

2–3 tablespoons freshly chopped coriander leaves

### FROM THE SPICE BOX

**WHOLE SPICES**

2 teaspoons (4 spice spoons) coriander seeds

½ teaspoon (1 spice spoon) cumin seeds

**GROUND SPICES**

½ teaspoon (1 spice spoon) turmeric, plus a pinch for rubbing into the fish

½ teaspoon (1 spice spoon) garam masala

*SERVES 2*

Place the fish on a plate, sprinkle with a little salt and rub in a pinch of turmeric from the ground spices and set aside.

Dry roast the coriander and cumin seeds from the whole spices and the dried red chillies in a hot frying pan over low heat for about 2–3 minutes or until the seeds turn light brown. Transfer to a pestle and mortar and grind to a fine powder. Set aside.

Heat some oil for shallow frying in a frying pan over medium heat and fry the fish for 2–3 minutes or until lightly golden, turning once, taking care not to break the fish. Leave to drain on kitchen paper.

In a saucepan, heat the oil over medium heat and add the onion, and ginger-garlic paste. When soft and lightly browned, add the dry roast spice mixture and the ground spices and cook for 1 minute.

Add the tomatoes and cook for 2–3 minutes or until the mixture reduces to a thick pulp. Add the tamarind paste, coconut milk and water and simmer for 5–6 minutes adding a little more water if necessary to keep the sauce from getting too thick.

Gently slide in the fish, add the malt vinegar and green chillies and cook for 4–5 minutes. Finish with a squeeze of lime juice and the chopped fresh coriander.

### Time-saving Tips:

• If you want to skip the frying of the fish, sprinkle the fish with a little salt and a squeeze of lemon juice, leave for 5-7 minutes and then rinse gently in cold water and pat dry before adding to the sauce in step 6.

• You could make the sauce and freeze it ahead of time and then fully defrost and add the fish to the dish when needed. The sauce is also good with prawns.

*Sereena remembers this dish when visiting friends – fish, freshly caught and cooked right in front of them!*

# Kaju Macchli

## Cashew Fish

1 tablespoon lemon juice

600 g (1 lb 3 oz) skinless haddock fillet (or any firm white fish), cut into large pieces

5 tablespoons oil

2 red onions, chopped

2.5-cm (1-inch) piece of fresh ginger, grated

2 garlic cloves, crushed

6 tablespoons natural yogurt

75 g unsalted roasted cashew nuts

2 green chillies, deseeded

¼ teaspoon salt

400 ml (13 fl oz) water

**TO FINISH**

2 tablespoons freshly chopped coriander leaves

¼ teaspoon freshly ground black pepper

1 teaspoon lime juice

**FROM YOUR SPICE BOX**

**WHOLE SPICES**

½ teaspoon (1 spice spoon) mustard seeds

½ teaspoon (1 spice spoon) cumin seeds

1 bay leaf

**GROUND SPICES**

½ teaspoon (1 spice spoon) turmeric

½ teaspoon (1 spice spoon) ginger

1 teaspoon (2 spice spoons) coriander

*SERVES 4*

Put the lemon juice in a small bowl with the turmeric from the ground spices and mix to a paste. Rub this gently over the fish and set aside for 10 minutes to marinate. Wash the fish gently under a running tap to remove any fish odours and drain and pat dry with kitchen paper.

Heat 3 tablespoons of the oil in a shallow frying pan over medium heat and fry the fish fillets on both sides for 2–3 minutes until golden. Remove with a slotted spoon and set aside.

Add the onions to the hot pan and fry for 4 minutes, or until soft. Add the ginger and garlic and fry for 1 minute, stirring frequently.

Put the fried onion mixture, yogurt, cashew nuts, green chillies, salt and the remaining ground spices in a food processor or blender. Blitz, adding the water gradually, for about 2 minutes.

Heat the remaining oil in a shallow frying pan over medium heat. When hot, add the mustard seeds from the whole spices. When the seeds begin to pop, add the cumin seeds and bay leaf and fry for 30 seconds.

Pour the blended mixture into the hot pan and bring the mixture to the boil, stirring frequently. Lower the heat and cook for 2–3 minutes.

Gently slide the fillets into the sauce, taking care not to break them. Cover and simmer for 5 minutes. Finish with a sprinkle of coriander leaves, some freshly ground black pepper and a drizzle of lime juice.

Serves with rice and peas, and lime wedges.

# Tandoori Macchli

## Tandoori Fish

600 g (1 lb 3 oz) firm white
   sustainable fish fillets (such
   as cod loin), washed
3 teaspoons lemon juice
2 tablespoons oil
2 tablespoons Greek yogurt
5 garlic cloves, roughly
   chopped
2.5-cm (1-inch) piece of fresh
   ginger, roughly chopped
2 green chillies, deseeded and
   chopped
1 tablespoon freshly chopped
   coriander leaves
1 teaspoon paprika
½ teaspoon freshly ground
   black pepper
1 tablespoon melted butter,
   for basting
Salt

**TO FINISH**
1 red onion, sliced into rings
Lime wedges
Mint and Yogurt Chutney
   (see page 17)

**FROM YOUR SPICE BOX**
**GROUND SPICES**
A pinch of (¼ spice spoon)
   turmeric
1 teaspoon (2 spice spoons)
   coriander
¼ teaspoon (½ spice spoon)
   garam masala
1 teaspoon (2 spice spoons)
   mango powder

*SERVES 4*

Drizzle the fish with the lemon juice and some salt and set aside for about 5–7 minutes.

Put all the remaining ingredients, except the black pepper and melted butter, with all the ground spices in a food processor or blender and blitz to a smooth paste.

Place the fish in a shallow dish and pour over the yogurt mixture. Turn to make sure the fish is evenly coated. Cover and set aside to marinate for at least 20 minutes (but no longer than 2 hours).

Preheat the grill to high. Cover the grill tray with greased foil and place the fish on this. Sprinkle with black pepper and grill for 3–4 minutes on each side or until golden brown. Baste with melted butter halfway through the cooking time before turning over.

Serve hot with onion rings, lime wedges, rice and the chutney.

**Variations:**
• Make a change to the Mint and Yogurt Chutney, by substituting the mint for coriander to make a tangy fresh coriander chutney.
• Cubed salmon fillet could be used instead of the white fish.
• This can also be cooked on a hot barbecue – just dot the fish all over with butter, wrap in a foil parcel and cook for 6–8 minutes.

*Even if you're not a lover of fish, this is an incredibly light dish and just fantastic!*

# Royallu Vepudu

## Stir-fried Ginger and Honey King Prawns

500 g (1 lb) raw king prawns, fresh or frozen (and thawed), peeled and deveined, tails left on

4-cm (1½-inch) piece of fresh ginger

4 garlic cloves

Juice of 1 small lemon

4 teaspoons honey

3 tablespoons oil

2 onions, finely chopped

1–2 green chillies, left whole and pierced

Salt and freshly ground black pepper

Lemon and lime wedges, to serve

**FROM YOUR SPICE BOX**

**WHOLE SPICE**

10 curry leaves

**GROUND SPICES**

½ teaspoon (1 spice spoon) chilli

¼ teaspoon (½ spice spoon) turmeric

½ teaspoon (1 spice spoon) coriander

¼ teaspoon (½ spice spoon) cumin

½ teaspoon (1 spice spoon) garam masala

*SERVES 4*

Place the prawns in a shallow dish and set aside until needed.

Put the ginger, garlic, lemon juice, honey, some salt and pepper and all the ground spices, except the garam masala, in a food processor or blender and blitz to a smooth paste.

Pour the paste onto the prawns, turn to make sure they are all well coated and set aside for 30 minutes to marinate.

Heat the oil in a shallow saucepan and add the chopped onions, green chillies and curry leaves. Fry for 3–5 minutes until brown.

Add the prawns and the garam masala and cook for 5 minutes (if using cooked king prawns, just fry for 2–3 minutes). Serve immediately with lemon and lime wedges.

**Variations:**
• The prawns can also be threaded onto skewers and cooked on a hot barbecue for 3–4 minutes or until cooked.
• The marinade can be cooked as in the recipe without the prawns and used as a sauce for fish or prawns.

# Malai aur Tamatar Jhinga
## Creamy Tomato Prawns

200 ml (7 fl oz) single cream or
 low-fat alternative
4 tablespoons tomato purée
½ teaspoon granulated sugar
3 tablespoons lemon juice
1 small green chilli, finely
 chopped
3 tablespoons oil
3 garlic cloves, crushed
200 g (7 oz) raw large prawns,
 peeled and deveined
Salt
Fresh coriander leaves, to finish

**FROM YOUR SPICE BOX**
**WHOLE SPICES**
½ teaspoon (1 spice spoon)
 cumin seeds
2 cardamoms, pods removed
 and seeds finely ground
½ teaspoon (1 spice spoon)
 mustard seeds
10 curry leaves

**GROUND SPICES**
½ teaspoon (1 spice spoon)
 chilli
1 teaspoon (2 spice spoon)
 garam masala

*SERVES 4*

Dry roast the cumin seeds from the whole spices in a hot frying pan over medium heat for 1 minute or until dark brown. Transfer to a pestle and mortar and grind to a fine powder. Set aside.

Put the cream, tomato purée, sugar, lemon juice, green chilli, ground roasted cumin seeds and cardamom seeds from the whole spices, all the ground spices and some salt in a bowl. Mix together and set aside.

Heat the oil in a shallow frying pan over high heat. When hot, add the mustard seeds from the whole spices. When the seeds begin to pop, add the curry leaves.

Lower the heat to medium, add the garlic and fry for 30 seconds, stirring all the time. Add the prawns and fry for 2–3 minutes on each side, being careful not to over cook them as this can make them rubbery.

Pour the sauce into the pan and then cover and simmer for 3 minutes. Finish with a sprinkling of coriander leaves and serve with rice.

*This is one of the fastest recipes we know! You can make it even quicker by using pre-cooked prawns and reducing the cooking time to just warm the prawns through.*

# Sabziyan

## Vegetable Dishes

*Avial*

# Mixed Vegetables in Coconut Milk

350 ml (12 fl oz) water

60 g (2½ oz) green beans, trimmed and cut into 4 pieces

60 g (2½ oz) carrot, cut into batons

60 g (2½ oz) sweet potato, cut into bite-sized pieces

40 g (1½ oz) potato, cut into bite-sized pieces

60 g (2½ oz) cauliflower, cut into small florets

60 g (2½ oz) asparagus tips, trimmed

1½ tablespoons oil

1 red onion, finely chopped

2.5-cm (1-inch) piece of fresh ginger, grated

3 garlic cloves, crushed

60 ml (2¼ fl oz) natural yogurt

1 x 400 ml (13 fl oz) tin coconut milk

2 red chillies, left whole and pierced

3 tablespoons freshly chopped coriander leaves

Salt

**FROM YOUR SPICE BOX**

**WHOLE SPICE**

7 curry leaves

**GROUND SPICES**

a pinch of (¼ spice spoon) turmeric

¼ teaspoon (½ spice spoon) cumin

*SERVES 4*

Put the water in a large saucepan, bring to the boil and add the turmeric from the ground spices, some salt and all the vegetables, except the asparagus. Cover and boil for 5 minutes, or until the vegetables are nearly cooked – al dente, but not soft. Drain and set aside.

Heat the oil in a shallow frying pan over medium heat. When hot, fry the onion, ginger, garlic and curry leaves for about 5 minutes until the onion mixture is lightly browned.

Mix together the natural yogurt and coconut milk until smooth and add to the pan along with the red chillies. Stir quickly to mix and make a smooth mixture.

Add the cooked vegetables and the cumin from the ground spices and stir to combine. Add the asparagus, cover and cook for 3-5 minutes, or until the vegetables are tender.

Finish with the chopped coriander and serve with rice and Stir-fried Ginger and Honey King Prawns (see page 84).

**Variation:**
• This also makes a wonderful soup – if you have any leftover, just put it in a food processor with some water to thin it out a little and blitz to a smooth consistency. Check the seasoning and serve. It can also be frozen in batches once made into a soup.

# Dahi Aloo

## Potatoes in Yogurt

4 potatoes, peeled and cut into
small cubes
125 ml (4 fl oz) natural yogurt
½ teaspoon salt, or to taste
200–250 ml (7–8 fl oz) water
3 tablespoons oil
½ teaspoon butter
1–2 green chillies, left whole
and pierced
2 tablespoons freshly chopped
coriander leaves
Freshly ground black pepper

**FROM YOUR SPICE BOX**

**WHOLE SPICES**
2 cloves
½ teaspoon (1 spice spoon)
cumin seeds

**GROUND SPICES**
¾ teaspoon (1½ spice spoons)
turmeric
¾ teaspoon (1½ spice spoons)
chilli
¾ teaspoon (1½ spice spoons)
fennel
½ teaspoon (1 spice spoon)
ginger
½ teaspoon (1 spice spoon)
coriander
A pinch of (¼ spice spoon)
asafoetida

*SERVES 4*

Cook the potatoes in a large saucepan of boiling salted water until just soft (test with a knife or fork). Drain and set aside.

Put the yogurt in a bowl and add all the ground spices (except the asafoetida), some salt to taste, 100 ml (3½ fl oz) of the water and whisk together until smooth. Set aside.

Heat the oil and butter in a shallow saucepan until hot. Add the asafoetida and the cloves and cumin seeds from the whole spices. Fry for about 30 seconds and then take the saucepan off the heat.

Leave the pan to cool completely before pouring the spiced yogurt mixture slowly into it.

Return the saucepan to high heat and bring the mixture to the boil. It is important to stir constantly at this point or the sauce will curdle. Add the cooked potatoes and cook for 5–7 minutes or until the liquid reduces.

Add another 100–150 ml (3½–5 fl oz) water, the whole green chillies and chopped coriander and mix together. Cover and simmer for about 3–5 minutes or until the potatoes are tender and some sauce remains.

Transfer to a serving dish and finish with some extra fresh coriander and freshly ground pepper.

Serve warm with basmati rice, Cumin Chicken (see page 56) and flatbread or naan as a side dish or as a snack.

**Note:**
• If the dish is left to sit for a while it may soak up all the liquid – add some more water before serving if necessary.

# Aloo Palak

## Spinach with Potatoes

225–250 g (7½–8 oz) potatoes, peeled and cut into bite-sized pieces 1 cm (½ inch) thick
150–200 ml (5–7 fl oz) water
300 g (10 oz) baby spinach leaves
3 tablespoons oil, plus extra for shallow frying
2 tablespoons tomato purée
½ teaspoon salt
2–3 tomatoes, peeled and chopped or 3 tinned plum tomatoes, drained and chopped
1 green chilli, left whole and pierced

**FROM THE SPICE BOX**

**WHOLE SPICE**
½ teaspoon (1 spice spoon) cumin seeds

**GROUND SPICES**
A pinch of (¼ spice spoon) asafoetida
¾ teaspoon (1½ spice spoons) chilli
½ teaspoon (1 spice spoon) ginger
½ teaspoon (1 spice spoon) turmeric

*SERVES 4*

Heat the oil in a heavy-based frying pan over medium heat. Fry the potato pieces for 10 minutes until they are golden brown. Set aside.

Boil the measured water in a deep saucepan and wilt the spinach leaves for 5 minutes. Drain through a sieve and collect the strained water for a later use.

Refresh the leaves with cold water. While in the sieve, mash and tease the spinach leaves with a spoon to break them up. Set aside.

Heat the oil in a shallow pan over medium heat and add the asafoetida from the ground spices and then the cumin seeds. When the seeds begin to pop, remove from heat and add the remaining ground spices, tomato purée and salt.

Return the pan to the heat and fry for 2 minutes before adding the tomatoes and fresh green chilli. Cook, stirring occasionally for a further 5 minutes to form a thick sauce.

Add the spinach leaves and mash against the sides of the pan to break them up further while stirring. Add the potatoes. Cook for 4–5 minutes stirring gently, taking care not to break up the potatoes, or until the potatoes are soft. Add the reserved water from the spinach if a runny sauce is preferred.

Serve with plain basmati rice and the Kashmiri Lamb Rogan Josh (see page 68).

# Sukhi Hari Rajmah

## Dry Green Beans

2 tablespoons oil

400 g (13 oz) green beans
  sliced finely at an angle into
  2.5-cm (1-inch) pieces

50 ml (2 fl oz) water

Salt

**FROM YOUR SPICE BOX**

**WHOLE SPICES**

½ teaspoon (1 spice spoon)
  mustard seeds

½ teaspoon (1 spice spoon)
  cumin seeds

**GROUND SPICES**

A pinch of (¼ spice spoon)
  asafoetida

½ teaspoon (1 spice spoon)
  chilli

¼ teaspoon (½ spice spoon)
  ginger

*SERVES 4*

Heat the oil in a shallow saucepan over medium heat. When hot, add the mustard seeds from the whole spices. When they begin to pop, add the asafoetida from the ground spices.

Add the cumin seeds from the whole spices and when they begin to sizzle add the green beans and some salt and fry for 5 minutes, stirring frequently. Add the water, cover and cook for 5–7 minutes, stirring now and then until the beans are soft and no water remains (add more water if necessary to continue cooking the beans). Fry for another 1–2 minutes.

Add the remaining ground spices and fry for 1 minute to blend all the spices with the beans.

Serve hot as a vegetable with a main meal.

*Lightly spiced and easy to make, this is a perfect accompaniment to any meal.*

# Bharwa Baigan

## Stuffed Baby Aubergines

1 small red onion

2.5-cm (1-inch) piece of fresh
  ginger

3 garlic cloves

1 green chilli, deseeded

2 tablespoons freshly chopped
  coriander leaves

1 tablespoon dark soft brown
  sugar

½ teaspoon salt, or to taste

2 tablespoons fresh coconut,
  peeled and grated (or dried
  coconut rehydrated in a little
  water or coconut milk)

8 baby aubergines, washed and
  patted dry with kitchen paper

2–3 tablespoons oil

Juice of ½ a lemon

**FROM YOUR SPICE BOX**

**WHOLE SPICES**

½ teaspoon (1 spice spoon)
  cumin seeds

¾ teaspoon (1½ spice spoons)
  coriander seeds

**GROUND SPICES**

½ teaspoon (1 spice spoon)
  chilli

½ teaspoon (1 spice spoon)
  turmeric

½ teaspoon (1 spice spoon)
  ginger

½ teaspoon (1 spice spoon)
  fennel

¾ teaspoon (1½ spice spoons)
  mango powder

*SERVES 4*

Dry roast the cumin and coriander seeds from the whole spices in a hot frying pan over medium heat for 1 minute or until they turn brown. Transfer to a pestle and mortar and grind to a fine powder. Set aside.

Put the roasted seeds, onion, ginger, garlic, green chilli, coriander leaves, sugar, salt and all the ground spices in a food processor or blender and blitz to a fine paste. Turn the paste into a bowl and add the coconut. Mix the coconut thoroughly with the paste.

Cut the aubergines from top to bottom without cutting all the way through to make a pocket. Fill the pocket with the blended paste.

Heat the oil in a heavy-based shallow saucepan over high heat. When hot, slide the aubergines gently into the pan and fry for 2 minutes. Turn the aubergines once and then lower the heat. Cover the pan with a lid and leave to cook for a further 5 minutes in their own steam.

Remove the lid and cook for a further 15 minutes or until the aubergines look slightly roasted.

Drizzle with lemon juice and transfer gently to a serving plate. Serve hot as a vegetable dish with a main meal or with flatbreads.

**Variation:**
• If you have any mixture leftover: fry the aubergines for 1–2 minutes and add the leftover spice mix with 300 ml (½ pint) water. Cover and simmer for 15 minutes, turning once, or until the sauce thickens.

# Tamatar Aloo

## Tomato with Potatoes

3 tablespoons oil

400 g (13 oz) potatoes, peeled and cut into bite-sized pieces

250 ml (8 fl oz) water

600 g (1 lb 3 oz) tomatoes, peeled and chopped or 1 x 400 g (13 oz) tin plum tomatoes, drained and chopped

1 green chilli, left whole and pierced

Salt

2 tablespoons freshly chopped coriander leaves, to finish

**FROM YOUR SPICE BOX**

**WHOLE SPICE**

¾ teaspoon (1½ spice spoons) cumin seeds

**GROUND SPICES**

1 teaspoon (2 spice spoons) chilli

1 teaspoon (2 spice spoons) turmeric

1 teaspoon (2 spice spoons) ginger

1 teaspoon (2 spice spoons) coriander

*SERVES 4*

Heat the oil in a shallow frying pan over medium heat until hot and add the cumin seeds. When they begin to sizzle, add the potatoes and some salt to taste. Fry for 7–8 minutes or until golden brown.

Remove the pan from the heat and add all the ground spices. Mix well with the potatoes and then add 100 ml (3½ fl oz) of the water. Return the pan to the heat over medium heat and cover with a lid for about 10 minutes, or until most of the water has evaporated.

Add the tomatoes and stir for 10 minutes, bringing all the ingredients together. Add the remaining water and green chilli, cover with a lid, and cook for 3–4 minutes, stirring occasionally and checking to see if the potatoes are tender. Add small amounts of water if further steaming is required. Finish with coriander leaves and serve hot.

# Shahi Paneer

## Royal Indian Cheese

2 tablespoons oil

1 tablespoon butter

1 red onion, roughly chopped

1 tablespoon Ginger-garlic paste (see page 15)

½ teaspoon salt, or to taste

1 teaspoon paprika

250 ml (8 fl oz) passata

1 teaspoon granulated sugar

1 tablespoon tomato purée

400 ml (14 fl oz) milk

250 g (8 oz) Homemade Paneer (see page 15) or shop-bought, cut into small cubes

1 tablespoon single cream, to finish (optional)

2 tablespoons freshly chopped coriander leaves, to finish (optional)

**FROM YOUR SPICE BOX**

**WHOLE SPICES**

½ teaspoon (1 spice spoon) cumin seeds

1 bay leaf

2 cardamoms, pods removed and seeds finely ground

**GROUND SPICES**

A pinch of (¼ spice spoon) asafoetida

1½ teaspoons (3 spice spoons) coriander

½ teaspoon (1 spice spoon) chilli

½ teaspoon (1 spice spoon) cumin

¼ teaspoon (½ spice spoon) garam masala

½ teaspoon (1 spice spoon) fenugreek

*SERVES 4*

Heat the oil and butter in a shallow pan over high heat until hot. Add the cumin seeds and bay leaf from the whole spices and the asafoetida from the ground spices. When they begin to sizzle, reduce the heat to medium, add the onions and fry for 5 minutes or until they brown.

Add the ginger-garlic paste and fry for 30 seconds before adding the remaining ground spices, salt and the paprika.

Fry for 30 seconds and then add the passata, sugar, tomato purée and the cardamom seeds from the whole spices. Cook for 3–5 minutes, stirring continuously. Remove from the heat when the sauce begins to thicken and some oil is visible.

Stir continuously while adding the milk to the saucepan. Return to the heat, bring to the boil slowly and then cover and simmer for 5 minutes.

Stir in the paneer and cover and simmer for 5 minutes or until the sauce begins to thicken. Remove and discard the bay leaf.

Finish with a swirl of cream and some chopped coriander, if liked. Serve shahi paneer with naan bread, chapati or rice.

### Time-saving Tips:
• Soak shop-bought paneer in boiling water for 10 minutes and then drain before using – this will soften the paneer.
• This dish can be frozen and fully defrosted and reheated as needed.

# Kadahi Gucchi aur Tamatar

## Pan-fried Mushrooms with Tomatoes

3 tablespoons oil

1 dried red chilli, left whole

1 onion, finely chopped

1 tablespoon Ginger-garlic Paste (see page 15)

300 g (10 oz) tomatoes, peeled and chopped

450 g (14½ oz) button mushrooms, washed and halved

¼ teaspoon freshly ground black pepper

1 green chilli, left whole and pierced

2 tablespoons freshly chopped coriander leaves

Salt

**FROM YOUR SPICE BOX**

**WHOLE SPICES**

½ teaspoon (1 spice spoon) coriander seeds

½ teaspoon (1 spice spoon) cumin seeds

**GROUND SPICES**

½ teaspoon (1 spice spoon) chilli

¼ teaspoon (½ spice spoon) ginger

¼ teaspoon (½ spice spoon) garam masala

*SERVES 4*

Dry roast the coriander seeds from the whole spices in a hot frying pan over medium heat for 30 seconds or until light brown. Transfer to a pestle and mortar and grind to a fine powder. Set aside.

Heat the oil in a heavy-based shallow frying pan over high heat. When hot, add the cumin seeds. When the seeds begin to sizzle, add the dried red chilli, followed by the onion.

Stir for 1 minute and then add the ginger-garlic paste and cook for a further 2 minutes or until the mixture is soft and translucent.

Add all the ground spices, except the garam masala, and some salt followed by the tomatoes. Stir to combine the mixture and to prevent it sticking to the bottom of the pan.

Add the mushrooms and cook over medium heat for 2 minutes. Stir, cover and boil for 5 minutes to reduce the liquid and thicken the sauce.

Stir in the black pepper, roasted coriander seeds and the green chilli and stir a few times. Stir in the garam masala and then finish with a sprinkling of the coriander leaves.

# Dum Sitaphall Rogan Josh
## Butternut Squash Rogan Josh

4 tablespoons natural yogurt

2 tablespoons tomato purée

A small pinch of freshly
ground black pepper

A pinch of cinnamon

4 tablespoons oil

800 g (1 lb 10 oz) butternut
squash, peeled, deseeded
and cut into 2.5 x 5-cm
(1 x 2-inch) chunks

350 ml (12 fl oz) water

1 teaspoon ghee or butter

Salt

**FROM YOUR SPICE BOX**

**WHOLE SPICES**

2 cardamoms, pods crushed
lightly

2 bay leaves

2 cloves, ground

½ teaspoon (1 spice spoon)
cumin seeds

**GROUND SPICES**

¾ teaspoon (1½ spice spoons)
chilli

¾ teaspoon (1½ spice spoons)
ginger

1 teaspoon (2 spice spoons)
fennel

¼ teaspoon (½ spice spoon)
garam masala

*SERVES 4*

Put the yogurt, tomato purée, black pepper, cinnamon, some salt and all the ground spices, except the garam masala, in a bowl and mix to a smooth paste.

Heat the oil in a heavy-based lidded saucepan over medium heat. When hot, fry the butternut squash for 5–7 minutes until golden brown. Remove with a slotted spoon and set aside.

Add all the whole spices to the hot pan over medium heat and fry for 30 seconds.

Add the yogurt mixture, stir for 1 minute before adding 100 ml (3½ fl oz) of the water.

Add the butternut squash, stir to combine and then add the remaining water. Lower the heat, cover the pan with foil and then seal with the lid. Simmer for 5–8 minutes, checking and stirring if required. There should be very little liquid and the butternut squash should be tender when cooked.

Finish with the garam masala and the ghee or butter mixed in. Serve with basmati rice, Rajasthani Chicken Strips (see page 54) and raita.

*Priya's favourite melt-in-the-mouth butternut squash, simply served with plain basmati rice... perfect!*

# Bindhi Bartha

## Stuffed Okra

500 g (1 lb) okra, washed and
  drained
½ teaspoon salt, or to taste
2–3 tablespoons oil
1 tablespoon lemon juice

**FROM YOUR SPICE BOX**

**WHOLE SPICES**

1½ teaspoons (3 spice spoons)
  coriander seeds
½ teaspoon (1 spice spoon)
  cumin seeds

**GROUND SPICES**

½ teaspoon (1 spice spoon)
  chilli
½ teaspoon (1 spice spoon)
  turmeric
1 teaspoon (2 spice spoons)
  coriander
¼ teaspoon (½ spice spoon)
  cumin
¼ teaspoon (½ spice spoon)
  mango powder
2 pinches of asafoetida

*SERVES 4*

Pat dry the okra with kitchen paper to remove any remaining moisture (it must be dried well or the okra will be slimy).

Dry roast the coriander and cumin seeds from the whole spices in a hot frying pan over low heat. Stir continuously for about 2 minutes until the cumin seeds begin to darken. Transfer to a pestle and mortar and grind to a fine powder. Remove to a bowl.

Add all the ground spices and salt, except the asafoetida, to the bowl of roasted spices. Add 1 tablespoon of the oil. Mix all the ingredients and spices well by stirring with a teaspoon or spatula.

Cut the tops off the okra and slit them neatly with a knife from about a thumb's length from the top to the bottom tip. Wearing marinating or plastic gloves, stuff the okra lengths on both sides with the spiced paste. Press together to close and place the okra on a plate.

Heat the remaining oil in a frying pan over medium heat. Add the asafoetida and then slide the okra into the pan. Fry for 5–6 minutes, turning slowly to cook on all sides.

Remove with a slotted spoon onto kitchen paper. Serve hot as a vegetable dish with dal and rice.

*Haak*

# Baby Spring Greens

4 tablespoons oil
A pinch of bicarbonate of soda
550 ml (17½ fl oz) water
400 g (13 oz) baby spring
  greens, washed and leaves
  torn into four (remove and
  discard the thick stalks)
1 red chilli, deseeded and cut
  in half, plus extra finely sliced
  red chilli to finish (optional)
½ teaspoon salt, or to taste

**FROM YOUR SPICE BOX**
**GROUND SPICE**
A pinch of (¼ spice spoon)
  asafoetida

*SERVES 4*

Heat the oil in a saucepan over medium heat until hot. Add the asafoetida and remove from the heat temporarily.

Mix the bicarbonate of soda with 50 ml (2 fl oz) of the water in a small cup and then add this to the pan along with the greens. Stir a few times and move the leaves in the water.

Add the chilli halves, salt and the remaining water and return the pan to the heat. Bring to the boil and then simmer and stir the leaves occasionally for 10–15 minutes or until the greens are tender and until the liquid is reduced by half.

Finish with finely sliced red chilli, if using, and serve hot with rice.

**Note:**
• The bicarbonate of soda seems unusual, but actually keeps the greens a vibrant green colour.

*This must be the simplest dish in the world. This is our favourite type of greens to serve with any spicy meat dish.*

# Maki Naryal Mai

## Baby Corn in Coconut Milk

2 tablespoons oil

2 tablespoons tomato purée

200 ml (7 fl oz) coconut milk

Juice of ½ a lemon

1 tablespoon freshly chopped
parsley or coriander leaves
(optional)

300 g (10 oz) baby corn

1 red chilli, left whole and
pierced

Salt

**FROM YOUR SPICE BOX**

**WHOLE SPICES**

5 curry leaves

½ teaspoon (1 spice spoon)
mustard seeds

½ teaspoon (1 spice spoon)
cumin seeds

**GROUND SPICES**

½ teaspoon (1 spice spoon)
chilli

½ teaspoon (1 spice spoon)
turmeric

½ teaspoon (1 spice spoon)
coriander

½ teaspoon (1 spice spoon)
mango powder

*SERVES 4*

Heat the oil in a shallow saucepan over medium heat. When hot, add the curry leaves and mustard seeds from the whole spices. When the seeds begin to pop, add the cumin seeds.

Fry for 30 seconds and then add the tomato purée, some salt to taste and all the ground spices. Stir well for 30–45 seconds and then add the coconut milk. Stir continuously and cook without boiling for 1 minute.

Stir in the lemon juice and either parsley or coriander leaves, if using, and then add the corn and red chilli. Simmer for 3–4 minutes or until the corn is tender and then serve.

**Variation:**

• It is also possible to make this dish with tinned corn kernels of a similar weight to the baby corn.

# Dal-chawal

## Rice, Beans and Lentils

# Curd Rice

## Yogurt Rice

250 g (8 oz) basmati rice,
   rinsed

750–800 ml (1¼–1⅓ pints)
   water

500 ml (17 fl oz) natural yogurt

½ tablespoon freshly chopped
   coriander leaves

1–2 green chillies, deseeded
   and finely chopped

1 tablespoon oil

1 tablespoon butter

2 dried red chillies

2.5-cm (1-inch) piece of fresh
   ginger, grated

3 tablespoons soured cream

1–2 tablespoons single cream
   (optional)

Salt

1 small carrot, peeled and
   grated, to finish.

**FROM YOUR SPICE BOX**

**WHOLE SPICES**

½ teaspoon (1 spice spoon)
   mustard seeds

3 curry leaves, plus extra to
   finish

**GROUND SPICE**

2 pinches of (¼ spice spoon)
   asafoetida

*SERVES 4–6*

Cook the rice in a large saucepan with the water following the packet instructions to make a softer rice than normal. Drain and cool in a large bowl.

Add the yogurt, coriander, green chilli and some salt to the rice. Stir well and bring together.

Heat the oil and butter in a frying pan over medium heat. When hot, add the mustard seeds from the whole spices. When the seeds begin to pop, add the red chillies, asafoetida, grated ginger and the curry leaves from the whole spices (in that order). Mix together and then leave the spiced oil to cool.

Add the cooled oil to the rice and stir a few times to combine. Add the soured cream and single cream, if using, to give a creamier taste and mix to combine.

Finish with the grated carrot and then leave to cool in the fridge for about 1 hour before serving. Serve cold with a spicy or sweet and sour chutney or pickle of your choice.

*We love to eat this when out on a picnic with Tandoori Chicken (see page 58) and Stuffed Baby Aubergines (see page 98).*

# Khichadi

## Mong Dal and Rice

250 g (8 oz) basmati rice,
  rinsed

150 g (5 oz) mong dal, split
  and hulls removed, soaked
  overnight and drained

1.5 litres (2½ pints) water

2 tablespoons ghee or butter,
  plus 1 tablespoon, melted,
  to finish

1 teaspoons oil

1½ tablespoons Ginger-garlic
  paste (see page 15)

1–2 green chillies, deseeded
  and finely chopped

3 tomatoes, peeled and
  chopped

2 tablespoons freshly chopped
  coriander leaves

Salt

**FROM YOUR SPICE BOX**

**WHOLE SPICES**

3 bay leaves

½ teaspoon (1 spice spoon)
  cumin seeds

10 curry leaves

**GROUND SPICES**

½ teaspoon (1 spice spoon)
  turmeric

½ teaspoon (1 spice spoon)
  chilli

½ teaspoon (1 spice spoon)
  cumin

*SERVES 6–8*

Put the rice, dal, turmeric from the ground spices and some salt in a medium-sized deep saucepan. Add the water and cook over medium heat, stirring frequently with a wooden spoon for 30 minutes, or until the mixture is soft and thick. Lower the heat if the mixture begins to bubble too much.

Put the ghee or butter and oil in a frying pan over medium heat. When hot, add the bay leaves then the cumin seeds from the whole spices. When the seeds begin to sizzle, add the curry leaves, stirring to fry and blend together.

Add the ginger-garlic paste, fry for 30 seconds and then add the remaining ground spices and the green chillies. Add the tomatoes and stir to combine for 3 minutes. Add the fresh coriander and mix.

Add the mixture in the frying pan to the saucepan of rice and water and stir for 2 minutes to evenly mix the ingredients with the spices. Finish with some melted ghee or butter. Serve hot and eat with a sweet and sour chutney, such as Tamarind and Mint Chutney (see page 134).

**Variation:**
• Garlic and ginger can be avoided and replaced with 3 pinches of asafoetida at the same time as the cumin seeds if preferred.

# Tarka Chana Dal

## Split Yellow Gram Dal

250 g (8 oz) chana dal (split
yellow gram), rinsed until the
water runs clear and soaked
in hot water for 10 minutes

1.5 litres (2½ pints) water

3 tablespoons vegetable oil

1 small onion, chopped

3 garlic cloves, crushed

2.5-cm (1-inch) piece of fresh
ginger, grated

3 ripe tomatoes, peeled and
chopped

1–2 green chillies, left whole
and pierced

½ teaspoon lemon juice

A handful of freshly chopped
coriander leaves

Salt and freshly ground black
pepper

### FROM THE SPICE BOX

**WHOLE SPICE**

½ teaspoon (1 spice spoon)
cumin seeds

**GROUND SPICES**

¾ teaspoon (1½ spice spoons)
turmeric

¾ teaspoon (1½ spice spoons)
garam masala

1½ teaspoons (3 spice spoons)
coriander

*SERVES 4–6*

Place the chana dal and the water in a saucepan over medium heat, stir well and bring to the boil. Skim off any froth that forms on the surface of the water with a spoon. Cover the pan with a lid and reduce the heat to a simmer. Simmer, stirring frequently, for 35–40 minutes or until the lentils are just tender, adding more water as necessary. When the dal has cooked through, remove the pan from the heat and set aside.

Meanwhile, heat the oil in a frying pan over medium heat. Add the cumin seeds and fry for 30 seconds or until the seeds begin to sizzle.

Add the onion, garlic and the grated ginger and fry for 4–5 minutes, or until the onions are soft and golden brown. Add the tomatoes and stir well to combine. Add all the ground spices and fry for a further minute. Add 100 ml (3½ fl oz) water.

Cook for a further 5–6 minutes, or until the oil separates to the surface and you are left with a thick pulp.

Bring the dal to the boil and add the onion mixture and the whole chillies, adding more water if required to loosen the dal. Bring to the boil, and simmer for 10–15 minutes or until the dal is soft but not mushy (the chana dal should remain partially whole).

Season to taste with salt and freshly ground black pepper. Stir in the lemon juice and freshly chopped coriander just before serving.

### Variation:

• You can also use split yellow peas in place of the chana dal and cook in the same way.

### Time-saving Tip:

• Soak the chana dal in hot water for a couple of hours or overnight before using. If you can use a pressure cooker or soak the dal in salted hot water for a couple of hours first, the overall cooking time will be reduced.

# Varri-Mut

## Pan-fried Black Turtle Beans

2 tablespoons oil

1 small red onion, finely chopped

1 x 400 g (13 oz) tin black turtle beans, rinsed and drained

½–1 teaspoon salt

50 ml (2 fl oz) water

1 red chilli, left whole and pierced

2 tablespoons freshly chopped coriander leaves

A squeeze of lemon juice

**FROM YOUR SPICE BOX**

**WHOLE SPICE**

¼ teaspoon (½ spice spoon) cumin seeds

**GROUND SPICES**

a pinch of asafoetida

½ teaspoon (1 spice spoon) chilli

¼ teaspoon (½ spice spoon) ginger

¾ teaspoon (1½ spice spoon) coriander

*SERVES 4*

Heat the oil in a heavy-based saucepan until hot and then add a pinch of asafoetida and the red onion. Fry until the onion is soft.

Add the beans and salt and fry for 5 minutes over medium heat. Add all the whole and ground spices and stir to combine.

Add the water and red chilli and cook for 2–3 minutes – the water should reduce to leave just 2–3 tablespoons. Finish with coriander and a squeeze of lemon juice before serving hot with rice or any flatbread.

**Variation:**

• You could use 150 g (5 oz) dried black beans instead of the tinned beans if you have more time to spare. Soak the beans overnight and then place them in a saucepan with 1–2 litres (1¾–3½ pints) water. Bring to the boil and simmer for 30–45 minutes, stirring occasionally until soft. Add more water if required. Then add the beans as you would the tinned beans above.

*We remember eating this in Kashmir, hot from the stove, sitting by the window, watching the snow falling.*

# Rasam

## Light Dal Sauce

1.5 litres (2½ pints) water
50 g (2 oz) split yellow peas or
  split pigeon peas (arahar dal),
  washed and soaked in hot
  salted water for 15 minutes
1 garlic clove, crushed
4 dried red chillies
3 black peppercorns
1 teaspoon tamarind paste
1 tablespoon oil
Salt
1 tablespoon freshly chopped
  coriander leaves, to garnish
  (optional)

**FROM YOUR SPICE BOX**
**WHOLE SPICES**
1 teaspoon (2 spice spoons)
  coriander seeds
1 teaspoon (2 spice spoons)
  mustard seeds
½ teaspoon (1 spice spoon)
  cumin seeds
5 curry leaves

**GROUND SPICE**
A pinch of (¼ spice spoon)
  asafoetida

*SERVES 6*

Put the water in a large saucepan with the split peas, garlic and some salt. Bring to the boil and cook for 15–20 minutes or until tender.

Dry roast the coriander seeds from the whole spices in a hot frying pan over medium heat for 1 minute or until browned.

Put 2 of the dried red chillies, the peppercorns and the dry roasted coriander seeds in a pestle and mortar and grind to a fine powder.

Put one-third of the dal, 50–100 ml (2–3½ fl oz) water the dal has boiled in, the ground spices from the pestle and mortar, tamarind paste and some salt in a food processor or blender and blitz for 1 minute.

Return this mixture to the saucepan of dal and bring to the boil. Transfer to a serving bowl.

Heat the oil in a frying pan over high heat. When hot, add the mustard and cumin seeds. When they begin to pop, add the asofoetida from the ground spices, the remaining 2 red chillies and the curry leaves.

Drizzle the oil mixture over the blitzed dal (rasam) in the serving bowl. Serve the rasam hot and in plentiful amounts; it should generally be served drowning out the rice. Garnish with chopped coriander, if using.

**Time-saving Tip:**
• This dish can be frozen and then fully defrosted and reheated as needed.

*This is one of the best dishes from the south of India and like all south Indian foods, is low in calories and full of taste.*

# Chutneys aur Raita

## Chutneys and Raita

# Boondi Raita

## Crispy Chickpea Raita

55 g (2 oz) gram (chickpea) flour
½ teaspoon salt
50 ml (2 fl oz) water
Oil, for deep-frying
250 ml (8 fl oz) natural yogurt, beaten
1 tablespoon freshly chopped coriander leaves, to finish

**FROM YOUR SPICE BOX**
**GROUND SPICES**
½ teaspoon (1 spice spoon) chilli
2 pinches of cumin

*SERVES 4*

Sift the flour, half the salt, the chilli and a pinch of the cumin from the ground spices into a bowl. Mix them well with a spatula.

Add the water slowly to make a smooth and pourable batter, similar to pancake mixture.

Heat the oil in a *kadhai* (see below) over medium heat. Test the oil to see if it is hot enough by dropping in a cube of bread – if it sizzles and browns quickly it is ready for frying. Pour 2–3 tablespoons of batter mixture at a time into a colander held over the hot oil and push the mixture through to create small balls. Fry the balls for about 1 minute, or until light brown and crisp. Use a slotted spoon to remove the balls and place on a plate lined with kitchen paper.

Immerse the balls in a bowl of hot water for 30 seconds and then drain.

Mix the yogurt, remaining cumin and salt together in a bowl until smooth. Add all the boondi balls and fold them into the yogurt. Garnish with coriander leaves, if liked.

Serve cold as a dip with a hot and spicy meal.

**Note:**
• A *kadhai* is a wok-like pan used in India. Use a wok or a deep frying pan if you don't have one.

# Lassun Chutney
## Garlic Chutney

1 tablespoon oil

1 bulb of garlic, peeled and cloves smashed with the back of a knife

3 red chillies, roughly chopped

½–1 teaspoon salt

1 tablespoon lemon juice

**FROM YOUR SPICE BOX**

**WHOLE SPICES**

½ teaspoon (1 spice spoon) mustard seeds

½ teaspoon (1 spice spoon) cumin seeds

*SERVES 4*

Heat the oil in a small frying pan over high heat. When hot, add the mustard seeds from the whole spices. When the seeds begin to pop, add the cumin seeds followed by the garlic.

Lower the heat and stir regularly to fry all the garlic for 1–2 minutes, until they are all equally browned.

Put the chillies in a food processor or blender with the salt, lemon juice, 4 tablespoons of water and the garlic mixture. Blitz for 2–3 minutes or until the mixture is well combined.

Turn into a small bowl and leave to stand for 10 minutes. Serve as the spicy part of a milder meal.

*Be prepared for the flavour hit!*

# Makhanphal Chutney

## Avocado Chutney

1 ripe avocado, cut in half and
  stone removed
1 garlic clove (optional)
1 green chilli, deseeded and
  roughly chopped
3 tablespoons Greek-style
  yogurt
1 tablespoon fresh coriander
  leaves
½ teaspoon salt, or to taste
Juice of ½ a lime

**FROM YOUR SPICE BOX**
**GROUND SPICE**
¼ teaspoon (½ spice spoon)
  mango powder

*SERVES 4*

Scoop the pulp from avocado into a bowl and mash it with a fork.

Put all the other ingredients and spices in a food processor or blender
and blitz for 1 minute or until a smooth mixture is formed. Add 50 ml
(2 fl oz) water if required to loosen the mixture.

Add the blitzed paste to the mashed avocado and mix together, adding
more salt if liked. Spoon the mixture into a serving dish and serve cold.

*A creamy dip with a kick!*

# Imle aur Pudina Chutney
## Tamarind and Mint Chutney

4 tablespoons tamarind paste
½ teaspoon freshly ground
   black pepper
6 tablespoons brown sugar
1 tablespoon sultanas or golden
   raisins
2 teaspoons dried mint
4 sprigs of fresh mint leaves
50 ml (2 fl oz) water
Salt

**FROM YOUR SPICE BOX**
**WHOLE SPICES**
2 teaspoons cumin seeds
4 cardamoms, pods removed
   and seeds finely ground

**GROUND SPICE**
1½ teaspoons (3 spice spoons)
   black rock salt

*SERVES 4*

Dry roast the cumin seeds from the whole spices in a hot frying pan over medium heat for 1 minute or until the seeds turn dark brown. Transfer to a pestle and mortar and grind to a fine powder.

Put all the ingredients, except the salt, with the roasted and ground seeds and the remaining spices in a food processor or blender. Blitz for 2 minutes or until a smooth mixture is formed. Add 1–2 tablespoons more water if required. Season with salt.

Serve cold with Split Black Gram Lentils in Yogurt (see page 44) and with other snack dishes.

*Sour tamarind mixed with sugar gives a lovely combination of sweet-and-sour chutney. Give it a try, especially with snacks.*

# Naryal Chutney
## Coconut Chutney

2 tablespoons chana dal (split yellow gram) or ready-roasted whole chana dal ready-to-eat

200 g (7 oz) fresh coconut, grated

2.5-cm (1-inch) piece of fresh ginger, grated

1 green chilli, deseeded

1 teaspoon tamarind paste

50–100 ml (2–3½ fl oz) water

1½ tablespoons oil

1 dry red chilli, cut in half

Salt

**FROM YOUR SPICE BOX**

**WHOLE SPICES**

8 curry leaves

1 teaspoon (2 spice spoons) mustard seeds

*SERVES 4*

Dry roast the dal in a hot frying pan over low heat for 2–3 minutes until lightly brown. Set aside.

Put the coconut, ginger, dal, green chilli, tamarind paste, water, some salt to taste and half the curry leaves in a food processor or blender and blitz for a few minutes until smooth. Put in a bowl and set aside.

Heat the oil in a small saucepan over medium heat. When hot, add the mustard seeds, red chilli and the remaining curry leaves and fry for 30 seconds or until the mixture begins to crackle.

Transfer all the spiced oil to the coconut mixture in the bowl. Add some more salt to taste and stir for a few minutes to combine.

Serve cold as a chutney with any meal.

# Mishthaan aur Sharbat

Desserts and Drinks

# Garam Nashpaati aur Aam
## Warm Pears with Spiced Mango and Shrikand

**FOR THE FRUIT**

200–225 g (7–7½ oz) tinned
  mango slices in syrup or
  natural juice, drained,
  chopped small and syrup or
  juice reserved
Zest of 1 lime
A large pinch of cinnamon
2 teaspoons lime juice
400–425 g (13–13½ oz) tinned
  pear halves in natural juice
1 tablespoon demerara sugar
20 g (¾ oz) unsalted pistachios,
  chopped
15 g (½ oz) flaked almonds,
  to finish

**FOR THE SHRIKAND**

500 ml (17 fl oz) thick-set
  natural yogurt
4–5 saffron threads, soaked in
  2 teaspoons warm milk
3–4 tablespoons caster sugar

**FROM YOUR SPICE BOX**

**WHOLE SPICE**

1–2 cardamoms, pods removed
  and seeds finely ground
*SERVES 2–3*

To make the shrikand: line a sieve with a muslin or very thin cloth and pour the natural yogurt into it. Leave it to drain for at least 6 hours or overnight in the fridge. Discard the strained liquid and tip the thick, solid yogurt into a bowl. Add the warm saffron milk and sugar and whisk to a smooth consistency.

To make the fruit: preheat the oven to 190°C (375°F), gas mark 5. Mix the mango, lime zest, cinnamon and cardamom together in a large bowl. Mix the lime juice with the reserved mango syrup in a separate bowl and pour into an ovenproof baking dish.

Place the pear halves cut-side up on top of the syrup mixture. Fill each pear with the mango mixture. Sprinkle over the demerara sugar and top with the chopped pistachios and flaked almonds.

Bake in the preheated oven for 15–18 minutes or until the nuts are lightly toasted.

Serve the shrikand cold with the warm pears and spiced mango. This can also be served with vanilla ice cream.

**Variation:**
• This is also good served with thick Greek-style yogurt.

**Time-saving Tip:**
• Make the shrikand the day before so that the dish is quicker to assemble if you are short of time, or just serve the fruits on their own with crème fraîche, cream or Greek-style yogurt.

*A healthy dessert that can be knocked up in minutes.*

# Chikki

## Indian Peanut Toffee

125 ml (4 fl oz) water

1½ tablespoons butter, plus
    extra for greasing

2 tablespoons molasses

100 g (3½ oz) dark soft brown
    sugar (or 150 g (5 oz) jaggery,
    grated)

200 g (7 oz) unsalted roasted
    peanuts, skinned

*SERVES 4–6*

Grease a small baking tray and set aside.

Heat the water in a shallow saucepan over medium heat. Add the butter, molasses and the sugar or jaggery. Stir continuously for 5–6 minutes or until the mixture reduces by half.

Test a drop of mixture in some cold water and check to see if it has reached the hard-ball stage – drop in a teaspoon of mixture, if it forms a ball and holds its shape it is ready. If it's not quite ready, continue to cook and reduce further and then test again.

Add the peanuts to the sugar syrup, stir vigorously for 45 seconds to prevent any burning to the bottom and sides.

Take the pan off the heat and pour the mixture evenly into the prepared tray. Press with a spatula or metal spoon to flatten.

Leave to harden at room temperature and then cut with a greased knife or break by hand when cool. Store in an airtight container for up to 2 weeks.

**Note:**
• Jaggery is a natural cane sugar and is available in Indian or Thai shops or can be bought online. If using jaggery instead of the dark soft brown sugar, leave out the molasses.

*Chikki is possibly the most popular sweet selling at every Chai-walla's and sweet shop, and if made with jaggery, it is so good for you too!*

# Nargal Roti Goan Ki
## Goan Coconut Crêpes

**FOR THE CREPES**

Butter or oil, for frying

125 g (4 oz) plain flour

¼ teaspoon baking powder

¼ teaspoon salt

1 egg

1½ tablespoons caster sugar

280 ml (9 fl oz) coconut milk

1 teaspoon vanilla extract

**FOR THE FILLING**

40 g (1½ oz) dark soft brown
   sugar or jaggery

150 g (5 oz) fresh coconut or
   desiccated coconut soaked in
   milk or coconut milk for 10
   minutes to rehydrate,
   and drained

**TO FINISH**

Desiccated coconut

Icing sugar

Strawberries or raspberries

Single cream

**FROM YOUR SPICE BOX**

**WHOLE SPICE**

2 cardamoms, pods removed
   and seeds finely ground

*SERVES 6–8*

Whisk together all of the crêpe ingredients in a bowl to make a batter.

Heat some butter or oil in a nonstick frying pan over medium heat and swirl the pan to coat. Take a soup ladleful of batter and pour it into the frying pan, swirling the pan again so that the batter coats the base of the pan.

Cook for 3 minutes and then check to see that the underside is light brown. Gently flip the crêpe over and cook for 1 minute. Stack the crêpes one on top of another, set aside and keep warm.

For the filling, put the dark soft brown sugar or jaggery, coconut and the cardamoms from the whole spices in a small shallow saucepan over medium heat. Stir vigorously for 3–4 minutes and then leave to cool.

Fill each crêpe with some of the coconut filling and then roll or fold. Serve the pancakes warm, sprinkled with desiccated coconut and icing sugar. Finish with strawberries or raspberries and a little single cream, if liked.

*This dessert reminds Alexa of her honeymoon in Goa.*

# Kesari Phirni

## Saffron Rice Dessert

600 ml (1 pint) milk
100 g (3½ oz) ground rice flour
40 g (1½ oz) granulated sugar
50 ml (2 fl oz) single cream
A large pinch of saffron
  threads, crushed and soaked
  in 2 tablespoons warm milk
2 drops of rosewater essence

**TO FINISH (OPTIONAL)**
Chopped pistachios
Flaked almonds
Caster sugar

**FROM YOUR SPICE BOX**
**WHOLE SPICE**
2 cardamoms, pods removed
  and seeds finely ground

*SERVES 4*

Put the milk in a heavy-based saucepan over medium heat and bring to the boil. Add the rice flour and cardamom seeds and then stir frequently to prevent any lumps forming.

Reduce the heat and cook, stirring continuously, for 4–5 minutes or until it coats the back of a spoon.

Add the sugar and cook for 1–2 minutes and then add the cream, saffron milk and the rosewater essence. Cook for a further 2 minutes, or until the mixture is thick.

Take the pan off the heat and pour the thick rice into individual dishes. Sprinkle with pistachios, almonds and caster sugar, if liked. Leave to cool and then transfer to the fridge to set for 30 minutes. Serve chilled.

*Traditional phirni is served in earthen dishes which resemble something like a mix of a plate and bowl – it tastes so much better and a little grit does no one any harm!*

# Lagan Nu Custard

## Celebration Custard

800 ml (1⅓ pints) whole milk
200 g (7 oz) caster sugar
3 eggs, beaten
½ teaspoon vanilla extract
2 drops of rosewater essence
½ teaspoon grated nutmeg
10 g (½ oz) flaked almonds

**TO FINISH**
Whipped or clotted cream
Rose petals (optional)
Edible silver leaf (optional)

**FROM YOUR SPICE BOX**
**WHOLE SPICE**
2–3 cardamoms, pods lightly
   crushed

*SERVES 6*

Put the milk and sugar in a heavy-based saucepan over medium heat and bring to the boil. Reduce the heat to low and cook and stir regularly for 20–25 minutes, or until the milk reduces by half. Take the pan off the heat and sit it in a large bowl of cold water to cool it quickly.

Preheat the oven to 180°C (350°F), gas mark 4.

Beat the eggs with the vanilla extract, rosewater and cardamom in a bowl. Pour this mixture into the cooled milk and then whisk together for 1 minute.

Pour into a greased 15–20 cm (6–8 inch) baking dish through a sieve and then sprinkle the nutmeg and almonds on top.

Bake in the preheated oven for 35–40 minutes, or until the surface turns golden brown.

Leave to cool and then chill in the fridge for about 1 hour. Cut into slices and serve with whipped or clotted cream. To make this extra special, sprinkle a few rose petals and silver leaf over the custard before serving.

**Time-saving Tip:**
• You can complete the first step and leave it in the fridge overnight, then all you have to do is finish with the flavouring and then pour into a tray and bake when needed the next day.

*This custard takes a little time but is worth it! It is delicious, light and creamy and keeps for a few days in the fridge.*

# Masala Chai

## Spiced Tea

1.5 cm (½ inch) piece of fresh
ginger, roughly chopped

2 tablespoons cane sugar (see
Note below)

2 tablespoons black tea
(caffeinated or decaf) – about
2–3 tea bags

2 twists of freshly ground black
pepper

200 ml (7 fl oz) whole milk

**FROM YOUR SPICE BOX**

**WHOLE SPICES**

4 whole cloves, crushed

4 cardamoms, pods lightly
crushed

2.5cm (1 inch) cinnamon stick,
broken into pieces

*SERVES 4*

Pour 750 ml (1¼ pints) of water into a small saucepan. Add all the whole spices and all the ingredients, except for the milk. Bring to the boil for 1 minute and then add the milk.

Half cover the pan and keep simmering the tea for 2–3 minutes being careful not to let it boil over.

Take off the heat and stir slowly once or twice. Fully cover the pan and then leave the tea to steep for 1 minute.

Pour into tea cups through a sieve and serve hot. Drink spiced tea with a light snack like Potato Chaat (see page 32).

**Note:**
• Traditional masala chai is made with cane sugar but you may use any sugar to taste or leave it out.

*Sereena and Alexa remember drinking lots of this tea on the train to Poona. The tea was sold at every train station. When the train pulled in, it was ready to drink!*

# Badam Thandie

## Almond Milkshake

40 g (1½ oz) ground almonds
500 ml (17 fl oz) milk
2 teaspoons honey
1 drop rosewater
5–6 ice cubes
3 saffron threads

**TO FINISH (OPTIONAL)**
Chopped pistachios
A few saffron threads

*SERVES 2*

Heat a frying pan over high heat. When hot, dry roast the ground almonds for 3–5 minutes, or until brown.

Put the milk, ground almonds, honey, rosewater and the ice cubes in a food processor or blender and blitz to a smooth consistency.

Pour the drink into tall glasses. Add the saffron threads, stir well and leave for a few minutes. Finish with a few chopped pistachios and saffron threads, if liked, and serve immediately.

*A healthy and delicious drink!*

# Milli-julti Phall Ki Lassi
## Mixed Berry Smoothie

1 x 340 g pack of frozen mixed
   berries (such as strawberries,
   raspberries and blackberries)
50 ml (2 fl oz) runny honey,
   or to taste
400 ml (13 fl oz) natural
   yogurt, stirred
A pinch of salt

**FROM YOUR SPICE BOX**
**WHOLE SPICE**
1 cardamom, pod removed and
   seeds finely ground

*SERVES 3*

Put all the ingredients in a food processor or blender and blitz to
a smooth consistency.

Pour into tall glasses and serve immediately.

**Variations:**
• Try varying the fruit and using a mix of frozen pineapple or mango or
just one berry, such as strawberry instead.
• The smoothie can be thinned down in consistency with milk, some
more yogurt or even coconut water (to give an extra antioxidant kick!).

*The colour of this smoothie is so inviting and it has
a heavenly taste. Frozen fruit makes this an easy
breakfast drink.*

# Index

# Author's Acknowledgements

Sereena, Alexa and Priya would like to thank their husbands, Norman, Jamie and Raj, whom without their love and support we could not have written this book. They would also like to thank Priya's daughter, Sinead and Alexa's daughters, Yasmin, Sophie and Priya, for happily tasting all the recipes and for loaning out their mother's for numerous Skype conversations across the continents between The Three Sisters!

To Mum and Dad, you know we could not have done this without you. Thank you.

The Three Sisters would also like to thank all at Simon and Schuster Illustrated, especially to Francine for believing in us, for her passion and enthusiasm and for helping to create The Three Sisters brand.

To Nicky, for her patience and support and to Ami for her continued encouragement.

We would also like to thank William, Liz, Kate, Corinna and Abi for their creative input in this book.

Finally, thank you to all our friends for endless cups of coffees, along with their help and advice.

*The Three Sisters*